The Ultimate Bread Machine Cookbook:

2000 Days of Simple, Cost-Effective, and Delectable Recipes | Clear Directions for Beginners to Craft Daily Fresh and Tasty Homemade Loaves

By:
Veda Clarke

Table of Contents

Introduction

A simple kitchen may be found at the center of every home, where the sound of laughing can be heard and lasting memories are created. It is a place where the clanking of pots and pans and the sizzling of various ingredients combine to create a symphony of tastes. But among all of the gastronomic marvels that come from this haven, there is one time-honored treat that occupies a special place in my heart: freshly baked bread. Imagine entering your home and being greeted by the welcoming embrace of warm, fragrant bread, its tempting perfume floating through the air as you enter the room where you prepare your meals. Our trip through the scrumptious landscapes of the "Bread Machine Cookbook: Embark on a Culinary World Tour Through the Aromas of Freshly Baked Bread" starts right here.

Have any of us not had an irresistible compulsion to enter a bakery at some point? The prospect of biting into that soft, pillowy interior can make our taste buds tingle with anticipation. The sight of properly risen loaves, with their golden crusts crackling with promise, and the mere thought of biting into those loaves can make our taste buds tingle. But let's be honest: the pressures of life have the potential to stifle our aspirations of becoming renowned pastry chefs. Our hectic schedules frequently steal both our time and our energy, leaving us wishing for the reassuring calm of home-baked bread yet intimidated by the prospect of the labor involved in making it. If you've ever had this yearning, or if you've ever wished for the gratification of serving a fresh loaf produced with your own hands to your family, then you are not the only one who has felt this way. The kitchen is a place of both happiness and difficulty, and I understand the agony of unfulfilled culinary goals that may have been hidden away among your obligations. The kitchen is a realm of both happiness and difficulty.

Your transformational trip begins here, with this cookbook serving as your guide and traveling companion. What if I told you that all the knowledge you need to create a wide variety of mouthwatering breads from different cultures around the world is right at your fingertips? What if I told you that you may now gain the mastery of a seasoned baker, not by spending hours upon hours in the kitchen, but rather by harnessing the power of a straightforward yet innovative piece of kitchen equipment — the bread machine? Your home can become a gateway to flavors from around the world with the help of this book, which contains the key to unlocking the world of bread-making. Your bread machine will serve as the vehicle, and your senses will be the ever-curious explorers.

When you start delving into the recipes in this cookbook, you'll find yourself on an extraordinary journey unlike any other. Imagine that you have mastered the art of making the ideal baguette, one that is reminiscent of a Parisian café and has a crust that breaks apart like a soft whisper. Imagine sinking your teeth into a substantial slice of Irish soda bread, the rustic appeal of which is a tribute to the bread's long and illustrious history. But why should we stop there? Imagine the unique combination of aromatic spices that go into making Indian naan, or the sweet memento mori that goes into making American cornbread, both of which have the ability to warm hearts with each bite. This book is not only about recipes; rather, it is about the art of making stories that weave together many cultures, flavors, and the power that freshly made bread has to bring people together.

I want to reassure you that this is not merely a collection of recipes in any way shape or form. It's a gastronomic adventure crafted specifically for the way you live your life today. This is about taking back control of your kitchen, reigniting your love for baking, and celebrating the symphony of flavors you can make with very little work. You will no longer be held hostage by the misconception that producing artisanal bread requires several hours spent kneading and proofing the dough. In the following pages, I will reveal the art of employing a bread machine, which is a kitchen buddy that is frequently underappreciated, as your ally in achieving bakery-worthy quality in your baked goods.

Why should you put your faith in me to lead you? My adventure into the world of baking has been full of opportunities for trial and error, as well as moments of epiphany. I have gained insight that I am anxious to impart as a result of the countless hours I have spent laboring over the creation of the ideal loaf. I've been through the trials that you might face, from sticky doughs to successful bakes, and I've condensed the lessons that I've learned into the core of this book so that you can benefit from them. My enthusiasm for baking bread has prompted me to investigate the bread-making traditions of various cultures throughout the world and modify old recipes so that they may be carried out in a contemporary kitchen. Not only am I an expert on the topic at hand, but I also consider myself to be a kindred soul and someone who has been down the road that you are about to travel.

If you've ever found yourself staring longingly at the displays in a bakery, if you've ever longed to discover the baker that lies dormant within you, and if you've ever dared to dream of baking bread that whisks your loved ones away to faraway lands, then you can be confident that this is the book for you. You are about to embark on a culinary world tour through the aromas of freshly baked bread, and the "Bread Machine Cookbook: Embark on a Culinary World Tour Through the Aromas of Freshly Baked Bread" will serve as your guide, your companion, and your passport to a world of delights. You will not only be able to recreate time-honored classics with each recipe, but you will also carve out your own story, one that speaks of your victories, your flavors, and the love that you inject into each slice. You will soon be greeted by the enticing scents of freshly baked bread; but, the question remains: are you prepared to go on this mouthwatering adventure?

Chapter 1:
Let's learn about Bread Machine

Bread machines are kitchen appliances that are specifically designed to bake bread. A bread machine will have a tin or bread pan inside of it that already has paddles constructed into it. They are arranged such that they are facing the center of the oven.

How does a bread machine function?

You will begin by inserting the kneading paddles into the pan. You will load the ingredients into the tin as the tin comes out of the machine, at which point you will also measure out the ingredients.

After that, all that is required of you is to put the pan in the oven (machine), adjust the settings on the electronic panel of the bread machine, and then shut the door. At this point, the enchanted bread machine takes control!

One of the first things that the bread machine is capable of doing is kneading the dough. It is possible to hear the sounds. If your bread machine has a window that displays the process of baking, you will be able to observe it all, which is a very interesting thing to do.

After the kneading process has been completed, there will be a period of relative calm, and then the growing phase will get underway. The bread machine facilitates the resting and rising of the dough. After that, there will be one more round of kneading, followed by the process of rising.

In the end, it will turn on the oven of the bread maker, and you will feel the steam coming up from the vent where the steam escapes.

What kinds of bread machines are there ?

The majority of the machines that make bread would look a little bit different from one another. This is because a bread maker is constructed to serve a particular function in each type of bread, which explains why this is the case. The following types of bread machines dominate the present market as the most sought after among consumers:

Vertical

As a result of the bread tin being created in this way, the majority of bread machines bake loaves that are inserted in a vertical position. In this style of bread machine, the kneading paddle comes in only one configuration.

Horizontal

In the pan of these bread machines are found two kneading paddles that are used to work the dough. These bread makers have the capability of baking bread in a horizontal shape, comparable to that which is sold in supermarkets.

Small

Small bread machines are ideal for households that have limited counter space or who don't consume a significant amount of bread on a regular basis. These helpful appliances for the kitchen do not take up a significant amount of space on the countertop and produce enough bread for two people or one person alone.

Large

It is helpful to have a large bread maker if you have a big family because bread tends to disappear quickly when there are a lot of people eating at the table. Large bread machines that can create loaves weighing 3 pounds each are capable of meeting the needs of a large family.

Gluten-Free

With such a wide variety of bread-making methods currently available, it should come as no surprise that numerous bread-making machines have been developed specifically to cater to the requirements of individuals who are concerned with maintaining a healthy diet.

How to use a bread machine?

Regardless of where you go or which bread maker you buy, the procedure of baking bread is essentially the same worldwide. After putting the materials inside of the bread pan, you place the pan inside of the bread machine and proceed to select the appropriate options.

The typical baking process takes anywhere from two to five hours, and this time span is contingent upon the type of oven being used. At the conclusion of the baking time, a loaf should be transferred to a wire rack so that it can cool completely before being consumed.

When making bread, you really need to include these four components.

- Flour
- Yeast
- Liquid(water, milk or any other)
- Salt

In addition to the primary components of the recipe, you are free to incorporate any other optional add-ons, such as chocolate chips, almonds, raisins, and other similar components.

Even while the process of making bread can appear to be quite simple and elementary, there are a few pointers that, when combined with a bread machine, will turn you into a bread-baking expert:

Check the manual and make sure you're following the directions. For certain bread makers, the dry ingredients should be included first, whereas for others, the order of incorporation should be reversed, with the wet elements going in first.

When reading baking recipes for bread, it is important to keep in mind that not all bread machines are created equally. Some make 1 pound, while others make between 1.5 and 2 pounds each hour. There are several configurations of the bread machine that have the capacity to bake loaves that weigh three pounds each.

When trying out a new recipe with the bread machine, it is essential to ensure that the quantities of the ingredients are comparable to those of the recipes that are typically used in the machine. It is imperative that the pan of the bread maker not be filled above its maximum capacity.

It is not recommended to use a delayed mixing period if the recipe calls for the use of milk in any capacity.

What kinds of bread can you make with a bread machine?

On the majority of bread makers, there is a wide variety of software to choose from, each of which is capable of creating a certain type of loaf. You can make whole wheat bread, white bread, or specialty loaves by employing different types of flour and modifying the other elements in the recipe. You can examine the various options that the bread machine offers by looking at the display screen on it (from the top: basic, whole wheat, multigrain, French, pizza, and bake only). When you want to make a different type of bread, all you have to do is put in a slightly different mix at the beginning of the process and select a different program from the list on the display. The bread maker will then automatically manage the various kneading, rising, and baking periods, and so on. (Therefore, the rising time for French loaves is increased, the preheating time for whole wheat loaves is increased, the kneading and rising periods for sweetbreads are increased, and the baking time for dark-colored crusty bread is increased.) Some bread machines even include a setting called "rapid baking," in which the loaf of bread is done in practically half the normal amount of time, although the overall performance is significantly less refined. Neither the increase nor the blend are quite as spectacular as they may have been. Baking bread is a process that requires patience and time; if you try to rush it, you can't expect picture-perfect results.

What else can you make in a bread machine?

1. The fact that most bread makers on the market now can also be used for other types of cooking is currently the best feature of these appliances. You are not limited to just making bread in a bread machine; in addition to bread, you can also make things like pizza dough and buns. With addition to bread, brownies, biscuits, and even cake can be easily prepared in a bread machine.
2. The majority of devices come equipped with a Jam function. Your bread machine may also be used to make delicious preserves such as jams and jellies. In addition to generating puddings and syrups, you may also use this setting to make ice cream. If the blade is positioned at the bottom of your bread maker, making scrambled eggs is a straightforward meal that can be prepared in a matter of minutes.
3. Therefore, there are a plethora of choices. You simply need to use your imagination.

Benefits of a Bread Machine

To begin, you are welcome to partake in the warm, handmade bread that has just been prepared. Bread machines typically come equipped with a timer that enables the baking cycle to be programmed to begin and end at specific times. This functionality is of great assistance whenever you want to receive some warm bread for breakfast in the morning. It may be done at any time.

You are able to exercise control over the food that you consume. If you bake your own bread at home, you have complete control over the ingredients that go into the loaf. People who are trying to limit their consumption of any of the ingredients, such as those who suffer from food allergies, will find this option to be extremely helpful.

Using a bread maker to create bread is a simple and straightforward process. Baking bread in a bread machine is a lot of fun, despite the fact that some people believe that cooking bread at home is a difficult task. You simply choose the program you want, and then you can sit back and rest. The bread maker takes care of the mixing, rising, and baking processes on its own, making the entire process incredibly tidier than it would be otherwise.

It will end up saving you a significant amount of money in the long run. You can be misled if you believe that purchasing bread at a supermarket would not break your budget. Baking bread at home will save you money in the long run, especially if you have dietary restrictions that prevent you from purchasing bread outside the home.

Bread machines have the capability of producing a wide variety of loaves, including gluten-free bread, rye bread, whole wheat bread, and hundreds of other types. In addition to making pasta dough, you can also make jam, pizza dough, and a wide variety of other delicious meals.

Is a Bread machine worth it?

You can get a bread machine if you need to produce a large number of loaves or if you desire an increased level of convenience. It's possible that you're sick of preparing bread by hand and that you lead a hectic lifestyle; if so, this machine is the answer to both of those concerns. Bread machines are quite simple to use, very handy, and ultimately worth every penny that you invest in one.

The price of a bread machine can range anywhere from $65 to $320 across the country. The amount of bread that you plan to bake will determine how long it will be until the costs of the bread machine are covered and you can begin saving money. If you have a large family that eats a lot of bread on a regular basis, baking bread at home is without a doubt the option that will save you the most money.

Bread machines, particularly more expensive models, were known to have a relatively long lifespan. There are individuals who have been making use of the identical bread machines for more than ten years.

Chapter 2:
Tips and Tricks

When you first begin to bake bread, you might believe that all you need to do is place the ingredients inside the pan, and the bread maker will handle the rest of the process. Even if this is a completely fair approach to begin baking bread, it is still a good idea to begin learning some of the techniques of the trade in order to obtain the greatest bread in your community.

Start Simple

It should not come as a surprise that starting with simple recipes is the greatest way to get your feet wet in the world of bread making machines. In fact, it is the best approach. If your great-grandmother produced the best bread in the world using 25 different spices and it took her over 24 hours to prepare it, you shouldn't be surprised if your first try at making the bread doesn't get the desired results. Test out some foolproof recipes and quick breads that are simple to make and call for a small number of ingredients. Even the recipes included in the bread maker's instruction guides aren't always successful. As you experiment with different combinations of components and determine which ones yield the best results, your ability to do so will improve.

There are some of the easiest recipes available online, and many times they are immune to negative reviews. Because of the proliferation of the internet, several of the best websites, such as Pinterest, now include sections where you can save recipes to use again and again. It is recommended that you take your time getting acclimated to the machine before attempting to bake breads that are not typically done in a bread maker. Because every machine is unique, it is important that you become familiar with yours before moving on to more challenging cooking techniques.

Be Cautious About Substitutions

Bread makers are particularly sensitive to even minute variations in recipe instructions. The bread you make now might not even resemble the bread you've produced in the past if you make even the smallest adjustment, like switching the sort of flour you use. This is due to the fact that various flours have varying amounts of gluten per unit of flour. For instance, as compared to bread flour, using all-purpose flour can lead to the production of a loaf of bread that is more compact in texture. Because flour is the primary ingredient in bread, even subtle shifts in the flour can be detected.

Also, give some thought to the yeast that you use in the recipes you create. In the event that the recipe calls for quick yeast, you should not use conventional yeast in its place. When it comes to preparing bread, yeast is one of the most challenging ingredients to master. To begin, you will need to determine the temperature at which the yeast will thrive. Any temperature that is too high will destroy all of the yeast cells, and any temperature that is too low will cause them to become dormant. Because of this, it is recommended to store yeast in the refrigerator. In most cases, recipes will additionally list the type and brand of yeast that was utilized in the dish. If at all possible, look for the exact same products.

Don't be Afraid to Peek

Always keeping an eye on your bread is a piece of advice that could be considered the most vital piece of this puzzle. There's a good reason why bread machines have windows, but it's possible that you won't be able to see the dough being kneaded inside. In addition to this, when the yeast develops, condensation will build up at the top of the machine, which will obstruct your view. It is not at all a bad idea to lift the cover and take a peek; in fact, this is something that you should do with every baking endeavor.

It is possible for paddles to get detached from their rotators, rendering them ineffective. If one half of your loaf is a brown mess and the other half shows promise, it is likely that your paddle was removed at some point during the baking process. Therefore, approximately ten minutes into the cycle of the bread machine, you should check to ensure that everything is spinning in an even manner. Check that the paddles are properly positioned so that they can turn while clicking into their allotted positions. When reaching their hands down into the machine, many people who make bread have experienced the jolt of discovering that there is no blade there.

After around ten minutes, examine the consistency of the dough to determine how the ingredients are coming together. Your dough will not properly cook if it is overly wet, and as a result, it will become crumbly and mushy. Fixes are available in the event that the dough has the appearance of goo and does not adhere to the other components of the dough. To remedy this issue, start by adding one tablespoon of flour at a time to the mixture and work your way up to the full amount. On the other hand, the bread dough could end up being far too dry once it has been mixed. The dough does not come into contact with the sides of the bread maker and instead remains in the middle of the machine. To correct this, add water to the machine in increments of one tablespoon at a time. A perfect piece of dough will not only form a ball but will also adhere to the sides of the pan.

In addition, check on the bread on a regular basis. Even while it is usually not a good idea to open the cover of the bread machine too frequently while it is baking, it is never a bad idea to take a quick peak inside to see how the dough turns out. However, if you open the lid too frequently, the top will fall, and your bread will no longer maintain the iconic form of sandwich bread.

Try the Dough Cycle

If you use the dough cycle of a bread machine rather than relying solely on the bread maker to complete all of your baking, you have a better chance of achieving fantastic results. This is despite the fact that it is easiest to simply add the ingredients to a bread machine and let it handle the rest of the process. There are bread machine experts who almost never turn to the baking procedure. They want their bread to have beautiful patterns on it or be topped with a glaze, both of which are impossible to achieve with a bread machine.

The crust is often considered to be one of the nicest features of freshly baked bread. There are hundreds of various types of bread, and each of those bread types calls for a unique set of baking skills. Some need to be cooked at a specific temperature, while others need to have the dough meticulously prepared before it can be baked. The crusts that are produced by a bread machine are typically very attractive, but they are lacking in the sophisticated processes that would make them more flavorful. Although bread machines include programs that can make the necessary adjustments, they are not able to accommodate every type of bread. However, rather of using a bread machine to produce the dough, you should attempt baking the bread in an oven.

There are a number of different dough cycles available, and the one you use will depend on the model of bread machine that you invest in. You have the option of either kneading the dough and letting the rising process take place naturally in the bread machine, or you can choose to let the machine handle the rising process on its own. Even while it may take a purist to simply allow the machine to do the mixing, there are still some people who only want the dough to be thoroughly mixed and have the appropriate consistency. For the rest of you, the fastest method for making dough is to utilize the quick cycle and then let it rise inside the machine.

If you have a machine that gives you the option to wait until the bread cycle begins before starting it, you need to make sure that your yeast is kept separate from any liquids that you will be using. It is imperative that you begin the mixing procedure as soon as possible after removing the dough from the refrigerator. If you want the greatest results from your bread maker, be sure to follow the directions.

Knead Dough After Dough Cycle

Do not beat the living daylights out of dough that has just emerged from the bread maker; nonetheless, it is a good idea to knead the dough for a minute or two after it emerges from the bread maker. By allowing the dough to rest, it will eventually become more malleable. You will be able to tell a difference in the quality of your dough even if you only knead it for a period of thirty seconds at a time.

Do Not Flour the Surface

If you are making bread using the dough method, you might choose to skip flouring the surface altogether. If you use an excessive amount of flour, your bread will turn out grainy and dry, which will result in a subpar end product for you. When you are working with dough, you should instead grease the surface of your counters. There will be no detrimental effect on the bread's overall quality as a result of the additional oils that are absorbed by the bread. If you coat your bread before placing it in the oven, you will find that the crust has a superior consistency after baking. In fact, this is one of the benefits of doing so. It's possible that the overall flavor of your bread will benefit from the addition of flavored oils. It is essential, however, that you do not pair unusual oils with unusual bread, as doing so will completely alter the flavor of the bread.

Additionally, using oil prevents sticky bread dough from adhering to your fingers, which is a major plus while working with it. If you have ever worked with dough that was too wet, you will understand what we mean by this. Because of the oils, both the bread and your hands will become slippery, which will prevent the sticky dough from catching.

Handle Dough Gently

After allowing the dough to rest for a while, you should take it back out and begin to knead it. Maintaining the surface tension of the bread with a moderate approach will result in a larger loaf of bread being produced. Fold the dough a few times and then gently push it flat on the surface you are using to knead it. After the process is complete, the dough can be molded into whichever designs appeal to you the most.

The next step is to place the dough in a warm area so that it may adequately rise. Allow it to rise for around twenty minutes before checking to see if it has reached the desired level of elevation. Test the dough by poking it with your finger; if it springs back up and then slowly slides back down, the dough is ready. If you are new to baking, you should experiment with different recipes and see which yields the best results for you. If you are unable to complete the baking process, you can store the dough in the refrigerator for up to twenty-four hours. While you wait for the allotted amount of time to finish baking, you are going to put the yeast into a dormant state.

Chapter 3:
Main ingredients

When it comes to baking, measurements are not merely a suggestion but an absolute necessity. On the contrary, it is scientific. When it comes to weighing the components, you need to have a lot of patience. For instance, if you want to outfit your kitchen with accurate measuring instruments, you should be sure to visit a store that specializes in kitchenware or shop online. Check that your equipment for measuring liquid and dry substances comes in a variety of sizes.

Among the most important mistakes that you must avoid doing again are the following:

Water

Water makes up the majority of the bread's liquid component. It is one of the essential components, similar to how flour is in the recipe.

Milk

After water, the most common liquid ingredient is milk, namely milk that has been seasoned with various kinds of herbs and spices. Just like the water, the milk that is used in bread recipes must be at a temperature that is lukewarm. This is especially important when the yeast and milk are mixed together.

Salt

When you are adding salt, there is one easy rule that you must keep in mind; you must keep it away from the yeast. In the event that the sugar assists in fermenting the yeast, the salt will put an end to the fermentation process.

Do not utilize the quantities of dry ingredients for liquid ingredients, and vice versa.

Both the dry and the wet measures of the teaspoon and tablespoon can be used interchangeably. On the other hand, cups are not. If you would like two cups of water, you will need to purchase two liquid cups. Do you not think there is any distinction between the two? Using a scale to measure a dry cup, fill the cup with perspiration, and then weigh the cup. After that, transfer it through the pipette into the liquid in the mixing cup. You will quickly discover that the computation does not provide an accurate result.

Flour

White flour is one of the goods that is used in the kitchen the most; it is without a doubt one of the most popular ingredients used in restaurants. Just consider how it is mentioned in practically all of the recipes: the word "flour" does not suggest entirely zero when used by itself. It would be the same as saying that you had to utilize meat in order to make a good broth: certainly, but which kind? You're going to end up with a flavorful stock if you use beef fillets. Excellent steak, however, for the love of God, it cannot withstand even the briefest amount of time in the oven. The same thing happens with flours; for instance, brioche flour, which is perfect for a recipe that requires a long rising time, cannot be used at all in the making of short crust pastry because it contains too much gluten. It will be a lot simpler to determine which type of flour works best for the preparation, and those who write the recipes will find this information much more useful.

The difference between soft wheat and durum wheat resides in the type of wheat that is used to make each type of flour. This is the primary distinction between the two types of flour. Flour made from durum wheat is noticeably more grainy to the touch than flour made from other types of wheat and is mostly used in the manufacture of pasta and some kinds of bread. The term 'durum wheat semolina' or 'durum wheat flour' may also be seen attached to the product being offered. On the other hand, the soft wheat ones are white in color, have a texture that can be described as practically "dusty," and are without a doubt the type that is utilized the most frequently in confectionary and bread manufacturing. They can be quite different from one another depending on the type of wheat that was used to produce them. The United States, Canada, and Argentina are the countries that produce the hardest soft grains, such as Manitoba and Plata. Um, amongst other things.

Flour is made up of many different compounds, the most essential of which are enzymes, Carbs, proteins, and mineral salts. This discussion will focus on flour's role in the culinary arts. When it comes to baking, enzymes are undeniably the compounds that are responsible for the most important role. These are then split into the amylase and protease categories. The first method uses the starch in the flour to provide the essential nutrients for yeast. On the other hand, the latter eats away at the gluten, which results in the gluten being more elastic. The sugars are utilized, which enables them to grow and mature into a food source for the yeast. Essential proteins can be broken down into two categories: soluble and insoluble. Gliadin and glutenin are the most important, and they are always discussed within the context of the culinary arts.

These proteins, dispersed throughout the dough, eventually come together to produce GLUTEN. In this context, it is important to note that there is a further signal, which is referred to as the W value. This value is used to refer to the 'power' that the flour possesses.

When compared to the results that follow, inferior flour and 'power' flour are classified as types of flour that fall into the following categories:

- Weak, with a maximum of 170 W. Cookie flour, waffle flour, breadstick flour, and several types of miniature baked goods. They must drink nearly half of their body weight every time they enter water.
- Intermediate: between 180 and 260 watts. dough that has been left to rise and requires a typical amount of water (or other liquids), such that used to make French bread, oil, or some varieties of pizza. They drink between 55 and 65 percent of their body weight in water and are the type of dough most commonly used in pizza restaurants.
- Powerful, ranging from 280 to 350 W. Bread can be made with a variety of flours, including those that require a substantial amount of water (or other liquids), such as those used in baba, brioches, naturally leavened pastries, and pizza with leavened dough. They drink approximately 65 percent of their body weight in water, which makes up 75 percent of their diet.

Types of Flour

Soft wheat flour: flour obtained from the milling of soft wheat, with thin, round granules, is the most frequently used flour in the method of making bread, and according to the rule, is the only flour that may be put on the market under the name 'flour,' accompanied by the form which, depending on the fiber and protein content, is defined by the following numbers: 00 (double zero), 0,1,2 and whole meal. Along with the 0, the 00 segregates the flour that is whiter but also contains the least amount of fiber and protein. This flour, along with the 0 segregation, is the one that is most frequently utilized in the preparation of bakery goods, not only in the domestic but also in the artisanal and agricultural contexts.

-

Flour from Manitoba: this type of flour, which is defined by a high quantity of gliadins and glutenin's, proteins responsible for the creation of gluten, has expanded with considerable success in recent years, as was already stated in the previous sentence. The milling of Manitoba grain results in the production of a unique variety of soft wheat seed that is mostly cultivated in a region of Canada (Manitoba) that was historically inhabited by indigenous peoples. The value of Manitoba flour lies in the fact that it is capable of producing a very robust leavening mechanism that is supported by an exceptionally sturdy and lightweight gluten mesh without requiring an excessive amount of kneading effort. The end product would be a loaf of bread that was exceptionally fluffy and aromatic before it was baked; but, after a few hours the bread would turn into an extremely rubbery consistency and would not be able to be stored for very long. The climate in Manitoba is perfect for leavening doughs, which, because to their high sugar and fat content, require a particularly extended length of rising time (panettone, baba, etc.).

The flours of type 1 and 2 are less expensive and more widely available; yet, they are wheat flours that are created by grinding the grain to a less refined degree. As a general rule, they are highly popular in the nations that are located in Northern Europe. Despite the fact that they are produced by milling wheat, they are able to reduce the amount of leavening that is required in some types of bread due to the larger weight that they possess.

Whole meal flour has the largest fiber content and outstanding nutritional value, despite the fact that its presence is the least pleasant. This is especially true for those of us who are from the Mediterranean.

- Durum wheat flour: semolina and semolina, which consists of coarse, glass-like granules and is primarily used for the creation of pasta, are utilized for the production of some traditional breads, particularly in southern Italy. This is the case.

- Spelt flour was widely utilized during the times of the ancient Romans. Spelt flour is characterised by a high number of mineral salts, which is the reason why its nutritious benefits have only lately been rediscovered. The manufacture of spelled is currently done primarily through the use of organic methods. Bread can be baked using this type of flour using only cereal, without any wheat flour being mixed in at any point in the process.

Rye flour, which is second only to wheat flour in terms of its prevalence in bread manufacture, is particularly popular in the German-speaking countries of Europe, as well as in northern Italy and South Tyrol. There is a summer variety and a winter variety, the latter of which tends to have more robust qualities where baked goods are concerned. Rye grain imparts a particularly unique hue and aroma to baked goods, in addition to being significantly heavier than the wheat flour that is normally blended with it. Because the gluten level is somewhat comparable to that of wheat, it is possible to make bread that is both very tender and very flavorful.

Corn flour is essential to the making of polenta and must be used. In some countries, such as Mexico, it is used in the same manner as wheat to produce the cooking of conventional tortillas, despite the fact that critical components like as calcium and a few vitamins are completely lacking. Because corn flour contains only a trace amount of gluten, if we ever decided to use it in the baking of any items, we would need to choose a corn flour that had a grain that was relatively fine and combine it with at least 45–50 percent wheat flour. Only then would we be able to use corn flour successfully.

-Oat flour contains a high concentration of nutrients and minerals; nevertheless, because it does not produce gluten-forming proteins, it must be blended with wheat flour to the following extent: In the process of producing bread, there should be 25 percent oat flour and 75 percent wheat or rye flour. It is also required to utilize oat flakes in order to make a lighter bread while still maintaining the proportions that were indicated previously.

The consumption of millet flour is particularly common throughout Asia and Africa. Despite the fact that flour enhances the flavor of food, it cannot be used on its own to make bread; rather, it must be blended with wheat flour of an exceptional quality in the following proportions: A mixture of millet flour and wheat flour that is 80/20.

The nutritional value of potato flour is quite similar to that of wheat flour; adding a small amount, about 20 percent, to wheat flour increases its leavening, flavor, and softness.

-Rice flour is the cereal that is richest in absolute starch and may be used to make bread; however, it needs to be combined with particularly strong wheat flour due to the fact that rice flour has an entire absence of proteins that enable gluten to shape itself (10 percent and 90 percent wheat flour).

Buckwheat flour is most commonly utilized in the cooking of traditional foods like pizzoccheri. However, when combined with wheat flour at a ratio of 10–15 percent, buckwheat flour can also be utilized in the production of bread. The bread is left with an unnaturally dark hue and a flavor that is just a touch on the bitter side as a result.

About The Yeast

Various Types Of Yeast

Yeasts are broadly defined as any substances that result in the dough fermenting into a product that has a greater volume after the process.

Beer requires yeast. This type of yeast is typically used for home baking and was historically derived from the residues left over from the fermentation of beer must. However, today it is produced from molasses, a by-product of the production of beet and sugar cane, and then compressed and sold in 25-gram home baking cakes and 500-gram skilled baking cakes. Home baking cakes can be purchased online. The 25-gram bread is assumed to be used because the word "panetto" is used interchangeably with it throughout the recipes. Be aware, though, that this is not a law that can be enforced!

Granulated or dried forms of brewer's yeast are also available, with the normal serving size being 500 grams of flour each sachet.

Wild yeast, often known as yeast mother. It is obtained by the prolonged fermentation of wheat and water, in addition to the addition of some fermentation-promoting agents such as yogurt, raw honey, or quite ripe berries, and it is useful for the production of certain types of bread and certain bread cakes (doves, panettone, etc.). It is also suitable for use in the preparation of certain types of bread. In most cases and according to the various recipes, the dough that has been fermented is put through a procedure that involves either refreshing or cleaning it.

Chapter 4:
Savory Bread

1. Cheesy Garlic Bread

- Cook time: 4 hours
- Servings: 16 slices

Ingredients:

- 5 eggs
- Almond flour, two cups
- Xanthan gum, ½ teaspoon
- Garlic powder, 1 teaspoon
- teaspoon of salt
- teaspoon parsley
- Italian seasoning, 1 teaspoon
- One teaspoon dried oregano
- 1 melted stick of unsalted butter
- 1 cup of mozzarella cheese, grated.
- Ricotta cheese, 2 tablespoons
- grated cheddar cheese in a cup

- grated parmesan cheese, 1/3 cup.

For topping

- ½ stick of melted, unsalted butter
- Garlic powder, 1 teaspoon

Directions:

1. Eggs are whisked in a bowl.
2. Put flour in a different bowl. All the cheeses and xanthan gum should be thoroughly mixed.
3. Put the butter in a bowl and season it with everything. Mix thoroughly.
4. Fill the bread bucket with the egg mixture. The flour mixture and seasoning mixture should then be added. Cover.
5. Choose the Low-Carb or Basic/White cycle setting. Click "Start."
6. When the bread is done, remove it.
7. Slice, let cool, then serve.

Nutrition:

- Kcal: 250
- Fat: 14.5 g
- Carb: 1.4 g
- Protein: 7.2 g

2. Cumin Bread

- Cook time: 4 hours
- Servings: 12 slices

Ingredients:

- 2 eggs
- 1 ½ tablespoons avocado oil
- 1/3 cup unsweetened coconut milk
- Picante sauce, 2 tablespoons
- almond flour, 1 cup.

- a half-cup of coconut flour
- ¼ teaspoon salt
- Baking powder, 1 tablespoon
- Mustard powder, ¼ teaspoon
- 1 teaspoon ground cumin

Directions:

1. Eggs should be beaten until foamy before adding milk, sauce, and oil.
2. Place the flour in a separate bowl, then mix and stir in the other ingredients.
3. The bread bucket should be filled with the egg mixture, then covered with the flour mixture.
4. Choose either the low-carb or Basic/White cycle. Click "Start."
5. When the bread is done, remove it.
6. Slice, let cool, then serve.

Nutrition:

- Kcal: 108
- Fat: 8.3 g
- Carb: 4 g
- Protein: 3.7 g

3. Bread With Beef

- Cook time: 1 hour 20 minutes
- Servings: 6

Ingredients:

- 10 g of beef
- 15 ounces of almond meal
- 1 onion and 5 oz. rye flour
- three tablespoons dry yeast
- Olive oil, 5 tablespoons
- 1 teaspoon of sugar
- Ground black pepper and sea salt

Directions

1. Pour the warm water into 15 oz. of the wheat flour and rye flour and leave overnight.
2. Chop the onions and cut the beef into cubes.
3. Once the onions are clear and golden brown, add the bacon and continue to cook for another 20 minutes on low heat, or until the onions are soft.
4. Mix the yeast with the warm water until it has reached a smooth consistency. Next, add the yeast to the flour, salt, and sugar, making sure to mix and knead the mixture thoroughly.
5. Mix well before adding the fried onions, black pepper, and beef.
6. The bread maker should have oil in it before adding the dough. For an hour, wrap the dough in the towel and set aside.
7. Put the lid on and select the basic/white bread setting on the beadmaker.
8. Only after the bread has been baked to a medium crust and removed from the oven, covered with a towel, for an hour, can it be sliced.

Nutrition:

- Carbs 6 g
- Fats 21 g
- Protein 13 g
- Kcal 299

4. Olive Bread

- Cook time: 4 hours
- Servings: 10 slices

Ingredients:

- 4 eggs
- 4 tablespoons avocado oil
- Apple cider vinegar, 1 tablespoon
- a half-cup of coconut flour
- Baking powder, 1 tablespoon
- Psyllium husk powder, 2 tbsp.
- 1.5 tablespoons dried rosemary

- ½ teaspoon salt
- chopped 1/3 cup of black olives.
- half a cup of hot water

Directions:

1. Beat eggs, and then blend in oil. Stir in vinegar and fold in the olives.
2. Place the flour in a separate bowl and mix in the husk powder, baking powder, salt, and rosemary.
3. Add egg mixture into the bread bucket, top with flour mixture, and cover.
4. Select the Basic/White cycle or low carb. Then press Start.
5. Remove the bread when done.
6. Cool, slice, and serve.

Nutrition:

- Kcal: 85
- Fat: 6.5 g
- Carb: 3.4 g
- Protein: 2 g

5.   Jalapeño Cheese Bread

- Cook time: 4 hours
- Servings: 8 slices

Ingredients:

- Greek yogurt, full-fat, 2 tablespoons
- 4 eggs
- a third cup of coconut flour
- Sea salt, ½ teaspoon
- Whole psyllium husks, 2 tablespoons
- Baking powder, 1 teaspoon
- Jalapenos, diced and pickled, ¼ cup
- ¼ cup of divided shredded cheddar cheese

Directions:

1. In a bowl, combine yogurt and an egg.
2. Put the flour in a different bowl. Mix well after adding the remaining ingredients.
3. Fill the bread bucket with the egg mixture, then cover it with the flour mixture.
4. Press Start after selecting the Basic/White cycle or low carb.
5. When the bread is done, remove it.
6. Slice, let cool, then serve.

Nutrition:

- Kcal: 105
- Fat: 6.2 g
- Carb: 3.4 g
- Protein: 6.6 g

6. Dill and Cheddar Bread

- Cook time: 4 hours
- Servings: 10 slices

Ingredients:

- 4 eggs
- Cream of tartar, 1/4 teaspoon
- 5 tablespoons unsalted butter
- 2 cups of cheddar cheese, grated.
- 1 and a half cups almond flour
- 1 scoop of protein from egg whites
- ¼ teaspoon salt
- Garlic powder, 1 teaspoon
- Baking powder, 4 teaspoons
- Dried dill weed, ¼ tablespoon

Directions:

1. Eggs, cream of tartar, butter, and cheese should all be thoroughly combined.

2. Put flour in a different bowl. Salt, garlic powder, baking powder, egg white protein, and dill are then added and mixed.
3. Fill the bread bucket with the egg mixture, then cover with the flour mixture. Cover.
4. Press Start after selecting the Basic/White cycle or low-carb.
5. When the bread is done, remove it.
6. Slice, let cool, then serve.

Nutrition:

- Kcal: 292
- Fat: 25.2 g
- Carb: 6.1 g
- Protein: 14.3 g

7. Yeast Bread

- Cook time: 4 hours

Ingredients:

- 2 Dry yeast, 1/4 teaspoon
- divided into 1/2 teaspoon and 1 tablespoon of erythritol sweetener.
- 1 1/8 cups of 100°F (38°C) warm water
- Avocado oil, 3 tablespoons
- 100 grams or 1 cup of almond flour.
- 35 grams quarter cup oat flour
- 100 grams soy flour
- 65 grams or half a cup of ground flax meal
- Baking powder, 1 ½ teaspoons
- 1 salt shakerful

Directions:

1. The bread machine, which can make a recipe for 2 pounds of bread, should be plugged in after gathering all the necessary ingredients.
2. Fill the bread bucket with water, whisk in the yeast and 1/2 teaspoon sugar, and let it sit for 10 minutes to emulsify.

3. In the meantime, take a big bowl, add the rest of the ingredients, and stir until combined.
4. It will take 3 to 4 hours to bake if you pour the flour mixture over the yeast mixture in the bread bucket, close the lid, choose the "basic/white" cycle or "low-carb" setting, and then adjust the baking time with the up/down arrow buttons on your bread maker.
5. Then, if a light crust option is offered, press the crust button to select it before pressing the "start/stop" button to turn the bread maker on.
6. Open the lid of the bread maker when it beeps, then remove the bread basket and lift the bread out.
7. After an hour of cooling on a wire rack, slice the bread into twelve pieces and serve.

Nutrition:

- Kcal 162
- Fat 11.3 g
- Protein 5 g
- Carb 7 g

8. Cauliflower and Garlic Bread

- Cook time: 4 hours
- Servings: 9

Ingredients:

- 5 eggs, divided.
- Coconut flour, 1/3 cup.
- 1.5 cups of rice and cauliflower
- Garlic, minced, 1 teaspoon.
- Sea salt, ½ teaspoon
- ¼ cup finely chopped rparsley.y.1/8 cup finely chopped parsley
- Baking powder, ¾ tablespoon
- 3 tablespoons unsalted butter

Directions:

1. Cauliflower rice should be put in a bowl and covered. 3 to 4 minutes in the microwave, or until steaming. then flush. Use cheesecloth to wrap and squeeze out as much moisture as you can. Place aside.
2. Egg whites should be whisked in a bowl until stiff peaks form.
3. Transfer a quarter of the whipped egg whites to a food processor after that. Cauliflower is the only additional ingredient. Blend for 2 minutes after adding the remaining ingredients.
4. Add the cauliflower rice, and blend for 2 minutes. Then add the remaining egg whites and pulse just until combined.
5. Fill the bread bucket with batter, then cover.
6. Choose the low-carb or basic/white cycle. Click "Start."
7. When the bread is done, remove it.
8. Slice, let cool, then serve.

Nutrition:

- Kcal: 108
- Fat: 8 g
- Carb: 3 g
- Protein: 6 g

9. Cheddar and Herb Bread

- Cook time: 4 hours
- Servings: 16 slices

Ingredients:

- 6 eggs
- Softened, unsalted ½ cup of butter.
- Almond flour, two cups
- Baking powder, 1 teaspoon
- Xanthan gum, ½ teaspoon
- Garlic powder, 2 tablespoons
- ½ teaspoon salt
- One tablespoon dried parsley

- Dry oregano, half a tablespoon
- 1 ½ cups of cheddar cheese, shredded.

Directions:

1. Eggs should be beaten until foamy before adding butter and combining.
2. Put flour in a different bowl. Add the rest of the ingredients and mix well.
3. Fill the bread bucket with the egg mixture, then cover it with the flour mixture.
4. Press Start after selecting the Basic/White cycle or low carb.
5. When the bread is done, remove it.
6. Slice, let cool, then serve.

Nutrition:

- Kcal: 207
- Fat: 17.5 g
- Carb: 5 g
- Protein: 7.2 g

- Cook time: 50 to 55 minutes
- Servings: 12

Ingredients:

- One-fourth cup coconut flour
- Cream cheese and eight eggs total.
- 2 and a half cups almond flour
- 50 g of butter
- 1 teaspoon rosemary
- Baking powder, 1 ½ teaspoons
- tsp of sage
- 2 tbsp. parsley

Directions:

1. Set the oven to 350 degrees. Using parchment paper, line a loaf pan.
2. Butter, parsley, sage, rosemary, and sour cream should be thoroughly mixed and made fluffy in a bowl.

3. Once all the eggs are incorporated and the mixture is smooth, whisk each egg into it.
4. A thick dough is produced by thoroughly combining the baking powder, almond, and coconut flour.
5. Fill the lined bread loaf pan with the finished dough.
6. For 50 to 55 minutes, preheat the loaf of bread on the stove. To make sure it is baked properly, check the center.

Nutrition:

- Kcal: 202
- Fat: 20 g
- Carb: 5 g
- Protein: 6 g

11. 3-Seed Bread

- Cook time: 4 hours
- Servings: 18 slices

Ingredients:

- 2 eggs
- Melted 1/4 cup of butter.
- 1 cup of warm (100°F) water
- Chia seeds, ¼ cup
- a half-cup of pumpkin seeds
- Psyllium husks, ½ cup
- Sunflower seeds, half a cup
- One-fourth cup coconut flour
- ½ tsp. baking powder and ¼ tsp. salt

Directions:

1. Eggs and butter should be thoroughly combined in a bowl.
2. In another bowl, add the flour. After that, combine all the ingredients—aside from the water—by stirring.
3. Then add the egg mixture, the flour mixture, and water to the bread bucket. Cover.

4. Choose either the low-carb or Basic/White cycle. Click "Start."
5. When the bread is done, remove it.
6. Slice, let cool, then serve.

Nutrition:

- Kcal: 139
- Fat: 10 g
- Carb: 5.6 g
- Protein: 5 g

12. Pumpkin Bread

- Cook time: 60 to 80 minutes
- Servings: 12 slices

Ingredients:

- 4 whole eggs
- 1 cup pumpkin puree
- 5 tbsp. unsalted butter/ghee softened
- 2 tsp. apple cider vinegar
- 1 1/3cup almond flour
- One-fourth cup coconut flour
- Flaxseed meal, 1/4 cup.
- Psyllium husk powder, 2 tbsp.
- Pumpkin pie spice, 1 tablespoon
- Keto baking powder, 1 tablespoon
- Sea salt, 1/2 teaspoon
- 1 cup acetate

For the glaze

- 1 tablespoon grated ginger.
- 1/9 cup water
- Xylitol 6 tablespoons, sea salt 1 pinch

Directions:

1. All the dry ingredients—aside from the sweetener—should be combined in a bowl.
2. Blend the butter and sweetener thoroughly. Add vinegar and eggs.
3. Fill the bread maker pan with all the ingredients. Put the cover on.
4. Choose Cake (bread machine time varies; 60 to 80 minutes).
5. Click "Start."
6. Once done, remove the bread and let it cool.
7. In a bowl, combine all the glaze ingredients.
8. Spread the glaze on top after the bread has cooled for 30 minutes.
9. Slice, then dish.

Nutrition:

- Kcal: 177
- Fat: 13 g
- Carb: 3 g
- Protein: 5 g

13. Cheese and Bacon Bread

- Cook time: 3 hours and 25 minutes
- Servings: 10 slices

Ingredients:

- Bacon dice, 7 ounces
- almond flour, 1 ½ cups
- Baking powder, one tablespoon
- Sour cream, 1/3 cup.
- two huge eggs
- 4 tablespoons of butter, melted.
- 1 cup of cheddar cheese, shredded.

Directions:

1. In the beadmaker, combine the flour, baking soda, sour cream, eggs, butter, and cheese.
2. Start by selecting White/Basic bread.
3. After ten minutes, check the dough.
4. After the beep, add the bacon.
5. When the bread is done, remove it.
6. Slice, let cool, then serve.

Nutrition:

- Kcal: 176
- Fat: 26.25 g
- Carb: 2.99 g
- Protein: 14.44 g

14. Vegetable Loaf

- Cook time: 4 hours
- Servings: 12 slices

Ingredients:

- 4 eggs
- Coconut oil, 1/4 cup.
- 1 medium zucchini, grated.
- 1 cup of pumpkin, grated.
- 1 small carrot, grated.
- a third cup of coconut flour
- almond flour, 1 cup.
- 2 tablespoons each of sesame seeds, flax seeds, sunflower seeds, and pumpkin seeds.
- Psyllium husks, 2 tablespoons
- 2 teaspoons of salt
- Smoked paprika, 1 tablespoon.
- Baking powder and 2 teaspoons of ground cumin

Directions:

1. Zucchini, pumpkin, and carrot are added after the eggs have been thoroughly beaten and are just combined.
2. Put flour in a different bowl. The remaining ingredients are then added and mixed.
3. Fill the bread bucket with the egg mixture, then cover it with the flour mixture.
4. Choose either the low-carb or Basic/White cycle. Click "Start."
5. When the bread is done, remove it.
6. Slice, let cool, then serve.

Nutrition:

- Kcal: 181
- Fat: 15 g
- Carb: 6.6 g
- Protein: 6.9 g

15. Lemon Poppy Seed Bread

- Cook time: 4 hours
- Servings: 6

Ingredients:

- 3 eggs
- 1 ½ tablespoons of melted, unsalted butter
- ½ a cup of lemon juice
- zested lemon, one
- 1 and a half cups almond flour
- Erythritol sweetener, ¼ cup
- Baking powder, ¼ teaspoon
- Poppy seeds, 1 tablespoon

Directions:

1. Lemon juice, lemon zest, eggs, and butter should all be combined.
2. Add the flour, sweetener, baking soda, and poppy seeds to another bowl and thoroughly combine.

3. The bread pan should now contain the egg mixture, the flour mixture on top, and a cover.
4. Press Start after selecting the Basic/White cycle or the low-car setting.
5. When the bread is done, remove it.
6. Slice, let cool, then serve.

Nutrition:

- Kcal: 201
- Fat: 17.5 g
- Carb: 2.8 g
- Protein: 8.2 g

Chapter 5:
Vegetable Bread

16. Cauliflower and Garlic Bread

- Prep time: 10 minutes
- Servings: 9

Ingredients:

- 5 eggs, divided.
- Coconut flour, 1/3 cup.
- 1.5 cups of rice and cauliflower
- 1 teaspoon minced garlic
- Sea salt, 1/2 teaspoon
- ½ tbsp. chopped rosemary, ½ tbsp. chopped parsley, and ¾ tbsp. baking powder.
- 3 tablespoons of salted butter

Directions:

1. Cauliflower rice should be put in a bowl and covered. 3–4 minutes in the microwave, or until steaming. then flush. Use cheesecloth to wrap and squeeze out as much moisture as you can. Place aside.
2. Egg whites should be whisked in a bowl until stiff peaks form.
3. Transfer a quarter of the whipped egg whites to a food processor after that. Cauliflower is the only additional ingredient. Blend for 2 minutes after adding the remaining ingredients.
4. Add the cauliflower rice, and blend for 2 minutes. Next, add the remaining egg whites and pulse just until combined.
5. Fill the bread bucket with batter, then cover. Choose the cycle marked Basic/White. Select START.
6. When the bread is done, remove it. Slice, let cool, then serve.

Nutrition:

- Kcal: 105.8.
- Fat: 6.8 g.

- Carbs: 2.3 g.
- Protein: 9.6 g

17. Vegetable Loaf

- Cook time: 4 hours
- Servings: 12 slices

Ingredients:

- 4 eggs
- Coconut oil, ¼ cup grate one medium zucchini, one cup of grated pumpkin, and one small carrot.
- a third cup of coconut flour
- almond flour, 1 cup.
- Pumpkin seeds, 2 tablespoons
- 2 tablespoons flaxseed
- Sunflower seeds, 2 tablespoons
- Sesame seeds, 2 tbsp.
- Psyllium husks, 2 tablespoons
- Salt: 2 tsp. Smoked paprika: 1 tbsp.
- Ground cumin and two teaspoons of baking powder

Directions:

1. Zucchini, pumpkin, and carrot are added after the eggs have been thoroughly beaten and are just combined. Put flour in a different bowl. The remaining ingredients are then added and mixed.
2. Fill the bread bucket with the egg mixture, then cover it with the flour mixture.
3. Choose the cycle marked Basic/White. Select START. When the bread is done, remove it. Slice, let cool, then serve.

Nutrition:

- Kcal: 178.2.
- Carbs: 5.1 g;
- Protein: 8.9 g

- Cook time: 60 minutes.
- Servings: 16

Ingredients:

- 30 ml of oil
- Three big eggs
- 1 1/2 cups canned pumpkin puree.
- 1 cup sugar, granulated.
- Baking powder, 1 ½ teaspoons
- Baking soda, ½ tsp.
- 14 teaspoon salt
- 3 cups of almond flour, ¾ tsp. ground cinnamon, 1/4 tsp. ground nutmeg, and 1/4 tsp. ground ginger
- Chopped pecans in a half-cup.

Directions:

1. Cooking spray should be used to grease the bread maker pan. In a bowl, combine the wet ingredients. Mix after adding each of the dry ingredients—all but the pecans.

2. Place the bread machine back inside after pouring the batter onto the pan. Select QUICK BREAD after closing. After the beep, add the pecans. When the bread is done, remove it. Slice, let cool, then serve.

Nutrition:

- Kcal: 52.4;
- Fat: 12.3 g;
- Carbs: 5.3 g;
- Protein: 11.6 g

19. Celery Bread

- Cook time: 3 hours
- Servings: 1 loaf

Ingredients:

- 1 (10 oz.) can of cream soup with celery
- 3 tablespoons heated low-fat milk.
- Vegetable oil, 1 tablespoon
- Celery, garlic, or onion salt, 1 ¼ tsp.
- sliced thinly fresh celery, ¾ cup
- 1 tablespoon fresh and chopped celery leaves
- 1 egg
- bread flour, 3 cups
- ¼ teaspoon sugar
- 1/8 teaspoon ginger
- Quick-cooking oats in a cup
- GLUTEN, 2 TBSP.
- Celery seeds, 2 teaspoons
- one package of dry active yeast

Directions:

1. All ingredients should be added to the bread maker.
2. Choose the basic bread option.

Nutrition:

- Kcal 70.2.
- Fat 2.6 g;
- Carbs 7.8 g.
- Protein 4.6 g

20. Pumpkin and Sunflower Seed Bread

- Cook time: 40 minutes.
- Servings: 10

Ingredients:

- Ground psyllium husk, half a cup
- Chia seeds in a half-cup
- a half-cup of pumpkin seeds
- Sunflower seeds, half a cup
- 2 tablespoons ground flaxseed
- Baking soda, 1 teaspoon
- 3 tbsp. oil, ¼ tsp. salt
- Egg whites, 1 ¼ cups
- 0.5 cups of milk

Directions:

1. First, put all of the wet ingredients in the bread machine pan.
2. Add the dry ingredients. Activate the gluten-free setting on the breadmaker.
3. Remove the bread machine pan from the machine once it is finished.
4. Before transferring to a cooling rack, allow to cool slightly.
5. The bread can be kept in the fridge for up to five days.

Nutrition:

- Kcal 150.5.
- Carbs 12.4 g;
- Fat 7.8 g;
- Protein 6.5

- Prep time: 25 minutes
- Cook time: 2 hours.
- Servings: 12

Ingredients:

- 1.5 cups of water
- 2 tbsp. plus 2 tsp. of unsalted butter
- 1/2 teaspoon of salt
- 1 tablespoon plus 1 teaspoon sugar
- Non-fat dry milk, 2 tbsp. plus 2 tsp.
- 4 cups of almond meal
- Active dry yeast, 2 teaspoons
- Dry onion soup mix, 4 tablespoons

Directions:

1. All ingredients—except the dry onion soup mix—should be added to the bread maker pan.
2. Put the lid on. On the bread maker, choose the BASIC cycle, then press START.
3. A ping will be heard from the machine after 30 to 40 minutes.
4. Add the dry onion soup mix while the bread maker is paused.
5. Press START once more to let the cycle run its course. Transfer the baked loaf to a cooling rack after it has finished.
6. Slice and serve as a soup side dish or with butter or cream cheese.

Nutrition:

- Kcal 326.8;
- Fat 14.9 g;
- Carbs 38.8 g;
- Protein 7.4 g

- Prep time: 10 minutes
- Cook time: 2 hours
- Servings: 10

Ingredients:

- 2.25 cups of flour
- Baking powder, 1 tablespoon
- 3 large eggs, 1 tablespoon of kosher salt
- a half cup of buttermilk
- Canola oil, 6 tbsp.
- 1 tablespoon dried basil
- 1 cup of roughly chopped sundried tomatoes.

Directions:

1. With the exception of the basil and sundried tomato, put all the fixings in the bread maker bucket.
2. Put the lid cover in place. Press START after choosing the QUICK BREAD setting on the bread maker.
3. Open the lid when you hear the ping, fruit, and nut signal, then add the basil and sun-dried tomato. Press START to begin, then place a cover. After the cycle is complete, place the loaf on a wire rack to cool.
4. Slice, then dish.

Nutrition:

- Kcal 180.2.
- Fat 4.1 g;
- Carbs 30.3 g;
- Protein 3.7 g

- Prep time: 1 hour and 25 minutes
- Servings: 10

Ingredients:

- 1 cup cooked and mashed sweet potatoes.
- Vanilla extract, 3 teaspoons
- Ground cloves, ½ tsp.
- Cinnamon, half
- Ground nutmeg, ½ tsp.
- 12 teaspoon of baking powder
- Baking soda, 1/4 teaspoon
- 5 eggs, ½ tsp. salt
- A half-cup of pure maple syrup
- 1 teaspoon oil
- 1 ½ teaspoons active dry yeast, 3/4 cup flour.

Directions:

1. Obtain a mixing bowl and add the flour, ground cloves, nutmeg, cinnamon, baking powder, salt, and soda.
2. The eggs, maple syrup, freshly mashed sweet potatoes, oil, and pure vanilla extract should all be combined in a different mixing bowl.
3. Pour the ingredients into the bread pan as directed by the machine's manual, paying attention to the yeast instructions.
4. Place the bread pan inside the appliance, choose the basic bread setting, the bread size, and the type of crust, if any, before pressing the start button after you've secured the lid.
5. When the bread is done, remove it from the oven and set it on a surface made of metal mesh to cool completely before cutting.

Nutrition:

- Kcal 91,
- Fat 1.59 g,
- Carbs 17.72 g,

- Protein 1.74 g

24. Onion Bread

- Cook time: 5 minutes.
- Servings: 6

Ingredients:

- 1 red onion, diced, cooked until golden with 1/2 tsp. butter.
- 3 teaspoons of melted unsalted butter.
- ¼ teaspoon salt
- Ground garlic, ¼ teaspoon
- psyllium husk flour, 3 teaspoons
- 5 eggs
- ½ teaspoon of baking powder
- Dry active yeast, ¾ teaspoon
- 1/8 teaspoon of onion powder
- flour, one cup

Directions:

1. Get a mixing container and combine the flour, salt, psyllium husk flour, ground onion, baking powder, and ground garlic.
2. Get another mixing container and mix the melted unsalted butter, eggs, and sautéed onions.
3. Pour the ingredients into the bread pan in accordance with the directions in the machine's manual, and then adhere to the yeast instructions.
4. Place the bread pan inside the appliance, choose the basic bread setting, the bread size, and the type of crust, if any, before pressing the start button after you've secured the lid.
5. When the bread is finished baking, remove it from the oven and let it cool completely before cutting and eating.

Nutrition:

- Kcal 124.7.
- Fat 9.2 g;

- Carbs 1.3g;
- Protein 9.4g

25. Beetroot Bread

- Prep time: 30 minutes
- Cook time: 45 minutes.
- Servings: 2

Ingredients:

- 1 cup freshly grated beetroot.
- almond flour, 1 cup.
- a half-cup of coconut flour
- 2 teaspoons of active dry yeast, 1/4 teaspoon ground cinnamon, and 1/2 teaspoon ground nutmeg
- Swerve sweetener, 1/3 cup.
- 50 ml of hot water
- 4 teaspoons of melted unsalted butter.
- Roasted and sliced walnuts amounting to 1/3 cup baking powder.
- 1/4 teaspoon salt

Directions:

1. Get a mixing container and combine the almond flour, coconut flour, roasted walnuts, Swerve sweetener, cinnamon ground, nutmeg powder, and baking powder.
2. Get another container and combine the warm water, shredded beetroot, and melted unsalted butter.
3. As per the instructions in the machine manual, pour the ingredients in the bread pan, taking care to follow how to mix in the yeast.
4. In the machine, place the bread pan, select the sweet bread setting - together with the crust type if available - then press start once you have closed the lid of the machine.
5. Utilizing oven mitts, remove the bread pan from the machine when the bread is done. After removing the bread from the pan with a stainless spatula, place the pan upside-down on a metal rack so it can cool before being cut into slices.

Nutrition:

- Kcal 852.4.
- Fat 41.4 g;
- Carbs 100.3 g;
- Protein 23.4 g

26. Tomato Bread

- Prep time: 15 minutes
- Cook time: 45 minutes.
- Servings: 1.5 lb./16 Slices

Ingredients:

- 4 whole eggs
- 2 tbsp. salted butter, melted.
- 1 cup flaxseed meal
- 4 tsp. oat fiber
- Baking powder, 2 teaspoons
- Xanthan gum, 1 ½ teaspoons
- Sea salt, 1/4 teaspoon
- 1/2 tsp. dried basil

- 1/8 teaspoon of garlic powder
- 2 tablespoons of diced sun-dried tomatoes
- grated 1/4 cup parmesan

Directions:

1. Whisk eggs and butter together with care. Fill the bread maker pan with all the ingredients.
2. Put the lid on. Depending on the model, set the bread machine's CAKE program for 30-45 minutes, and select LIGHT for the crust color. Select START. If required, knead the dough with a spatula in the breadmaker. Add grated parmesan to the top before the baking mode starts.
3. Use a toothpick to test the doneness after 20 minutes of baking. When the program is finished, remove the bucket and leave it outside to cool for 5–10 minutes.
4. Shake the loaf out of the pan and place it on a cooling rack to cool for 30 minutes.
5. Slice, then dish.

Nutrition:

- Kcal 87.8;
- Carbs 2.2 g;
- Fat 5.1 g

27. Zucchini Lemon Bread

- Prep time: 5 minutes
- Cook time: 40 minutes.
- Servings: 12

Ingredients:

- Almond flour, two cups
- Salt, ¾ tsp., and baking powder, 1 tsp.
- Baking soda, ½ tsp.
- 2 cups grated zucchini.
- Vanilla extract, 2 teaspoons
- Swerve sweetener, 2 lemon zest, and 1/3 cup.
- 3 eggs

- Melted 3/4 cup unsalted butter.
- 2 tablespoons fresh lemon juice
- Dry active yeast, 1 ½ teaspoons

Directions:

1. Almond flour, salt, baking soda, and baking powder should all be combined in a mixing bowl.
2. In a different mixing bowl, combine the shredded zucchini, unsalted melted butter, pure vanilla extract, lemon zest, and juice.
3. Pour the ingredients into the bread pan in accordance with the machine's instructions, being careful to follow the directions for incorporating the yeast.
4. Place the bread pan inside the machine, choose the basic bread setting, the bread size, and the type of crust, if any, before pressing the start button after you've secured the lid.
5. Utilizing oven mitts, remove the bread pan from the machine when the bread is done. After removing the bread from the pan with a stainless spatula, place the pan upside-down on a metal rack so it can cool before being cut into slices.

Nutrition:

- Kcal 228.7;
- Fat 15.7g;
- Carbs 14.2 g;
- Protein 3.5 g

28. Carrot Bread

- Prep time: 2h 10 Mins
- Servings: 1 loaf / 8 slices

Ingredients:

- 4 eggs
- ¼ teaspoon kosher salt
- ½ cup (4 oz) butter
- ½ cup (4 oz) sugar
- 1 tablespoon vanilla sugar

- 2 teaspoon cinnamon
- 3.5 cups of all-purpose flour
- 1 teaspoon of baking soda
- ¼ cup chopped nuts.
- ¼ cup grated carrot

Directions:

1. Put all the ingredients into the breadmaker as directed by the manufacturer (except the carrot). Set the LIGHT crust type and the CAKE/SWEET program in the bread maker.
2. Select START. Add a grated carrot after the machine beeps. Take the bucket outside after the cycle is finished so the loaf can cool for five minutes.
3. Slice the loaf, place on a cooling rack, and serve after gently shaking the bucket to release the loaf. Enjoy!

Nutrition:

- Kcal 395.8.
- Fat 15.7 g;
- Carbs 52.3 g;
- Protein 10.2 g

29. Zucchini Bread

- Prep time: 2h 10 Mins
- Servings: 1 loaf / 8 slices

Ingredients:

- 2 eggs
- 4 grains of salt
- oil, one cup
- White sugar, 1 cup.
- 1 tablespoon sugar with vanilla
- two cinnamon sticks
- 3 cups of well-sifted all-purpose flour and a half cup of ground nuts
- 1 teaspoon of baking soda

- Grated zucchini, 1 ¼ cups

Directions:

1. Put all the ingredients into the bread maker as directed by the manufacturer (except the zucchini).
2. Set the LIGHT crust type and the CAKE/SWEET program in the bread maker.
3. Select START. Add the zucchini after the machine beeps. Take the bucket outside after the cycle is finished so the loaf can cool for five minutes.
4. Slice the loaf, place on a cooling rack, and serve after gently shaking the bucket to release the loaf.

Nutrition:

- Kcal 555.6.
- Fat 30.1g;
- Carbs 62.3 g;
- Protein 9.6 g

- Cook time: 4 hours.
- Servings: 1 ½ pound 12 slices

Ingredients:

- 2 pasteurized eggs.
- 1 mug of butter
- 1.3 cups of sugar
- 1/3 cup of pureed pumpkin
- Ground 1/8 tsp. ginger
- ½ tsp. cinnamon
- 1/8 tsp. cloves, and 1 tsp. baking powder
- Ground nutmeg, ½ tsp.

Directions:

1. The remaining ingredients should be beaten until combined in a large bowl after the eggs have been cracked.
2. It will take 3–4 hours to bake the bread after adding the batter, closing the lid, choosing the basic/white cycle setting, and pressing the UP/DOWN arrow buttons to change the baking time.
3. Then, if there is a light crust option, press the crust button to select it before pressing the START/STOP button to turn on the bread maker.
4. Open the lid, remove the breadbasket, and lift the bread when the bread maker beeps.
5. Slice the bread into 12 pieces after it has cooled on a wire rack for an hour.

Nutrition:

- Kcal: 148.2.
- Fat: 12.9 g ;
- Carbs: 7 g ;
- Fiber: 2 g;
- Protein: 6.7 g

Chapter 6:
Mediterranean Bread

- Prep time: 15 min
- Cook time: 2 hours.
- Serving: 1 loaf

Ingredients:

- 2 cups of general-purpose flour
- 1-cup of hot water
- 1 package dry active yeast
- Extra virgin olive oil, ¼ cup
- chopped half a cup of pitted Kalamata olives.
- Oregano, dried, 1 teaspoon
- sea salt, one teaspoon

Directions:

1. Warm water and yeast should be combined in a bowl, and the mixture should sit for five minutes until foamy.
2. Sea salt, oregano, olives, and olive oil should all be combined.
3. Add the flour little by little and knead the dough until it is elastic and smooth.
4. The dough should rise in a warm location with a cover for about an hour, or until it has doubled in size.
5. Set your breadmaker to the Basic or White Bread setting to preheat.
6. The dough should be pounded down and shaped to fit the bread pan.
7. The dough should rise for an additional 30 minutes after being placed in the pan.
8. The bread should be baked in the bread maker until golden brown.
9. Prior to slicing, let the bread cool.

Nutritional Information:

- Kcal: 180
- Protein: 4g

- Fat: 8g
- Carbs: 23g

32. Rosemary and Olive Oil Focaccia

- Prep time: 20 min
- Cook time: 1 hour
- Serving: 12 servings

Ingredients:

- 3 cups regular flour
- 1-cup of hot water
- 1 package dry active yeast
- Extra virgin olive oil, ¼ cup.
- 2 tablespoons chopped fresh rosemary.
- sea salt, one teaspoon
- Topping salt, coarse

Directions:

1. For five minutes, proof the yeast in warm water.
2. 2 tablespoons of olive oil, rosemary, and sea salt should be combined.
3. Add the flour little by little while kneading the dough until it's smooth.
4. The dough should rise covered for about an hour, or until it has doubled in size.
5. Set your breadmaker to the Dough or Manual setting to preheat.
6. With your fingers, press the dough into a baking pan that has been greased.
7. Sprinkle coarse salt on top of the dough and drizzle the remaining olive oil over it.
8. The dough should be covered and rested for 15 minutes.
9. The focaccia should be baked in a hot oven until golden brown.
10. Before slicing and serving, allow to cool slightly.

Nutritional Information:

- Kcal: 180
- Protein: 4g
- Fat: 6g

- Carbs: 28g

33. Za'atar and Olive Oil Pita Bread

- Prep time: 20 min
- Cook time: 15 min.
- Serving: 8 pitas

Ingredients:

- 2 ½ cups of bread flour
- 1-cup of hot water
- 1 package dry active yeast
- Olive oil, 1/4 cup.
- 2 tablespoons of the spice mixture za'atar
- sea salt, one teaspoon

Directions:

1. For five minutes, proof the yeast in warm water.
2. Add the sea salt, olive oil, and za'atar spice mixture.
3. Add the bread flour gradually while kneading the dough until it is smooth.
4. It will take the dough about an hour to double in size after being covered and rising.
5. Set your breadmaker to the Dough or Manual setting to preheat.
6. Make eight equal portions of the dough into balls.
7. Each ball is rolled out into a flat disc.
8. Set a skillet to medium-high heat to pre-heat.
9. On the skillet, toast the pita bread for about 2 minutes on each side.
10. Serve hot.

Nutritional Information:

- Kcal: 180
- Protein: 4g
- Fat: 6g
- Carbs: 28g

- Prep time: 25 min
- Cook time: 25 min.
- Serving: 1 loaf

Ingredients:

- bread flour, 3 cups
- 1-cup of hot water
- 1 package dry active yeast
- Olive oil, 1/4 cup.
- 2 tablespoons chopped fresh basil, 1/2 cup chopped mixed Mediterranean olives, and 1 teaspoon dried thyme.
- 50 ml of sea salt

Directions:

1. The yeast should be dissolved in warm water and given five minutes to proof.
2. Add the sea salt, fresh basil, dried thyme, and chopped olives to the mixture.
3. Add the bread flour gradually while kneading the dough until it is smooth.

61

4. For about an hour, the dough should rise covered until it has doubled in size.
5. Set your breadmaker to the Dough or Manual setting to preheat.
6. The dough is shaped before being placed on a baking sheet.
7. Another 30 minutes should pass while the dough rises on the baking sheet.
8. Bake the ciabatta in a preheated oven until it turns golden.
9. Prior to slicing, let the bread cool.

Nutritional Information:

- Kcal: 190
- Protein: 5g
- Fat: 7g
- Carbs: 27g

35. Greek Yogurt and Honey Flatbread

- Prep time: 15 min
- Cook time: 20 min.
- Serving: 6 pieces

Ingredients:

- two cups of whole wheat flour
- Greek yogurt, half a cup
- 2 tablespoons of honey, 1/4 cup warm water, and 1 teaspoon baking powder.
- 0.5 teaspoons of salt

Directions:

1. In a bowl, combine the Greek yogurt, honey, and warm water.
2. Mix the whole wheat flour, baking soda, and salt in a separate bowl.
3. To make a dough, combine the dry ingredients with the wet ones.
4. Create six equal portions of dough, and then divide each into six balls.
5. Heat a flatbread pan or skillet to medium.
6. Each ball is rolled out into a flat disc.
7. The flatbread should be cooked in the heated skillet until spots of golden-brown color appear.
8. Cook the other side by flipping.

9. Serve hot.

Nutritional Information:

- Kcal: 160
- Protein: 5g
- Fat: 1g
- Carbs: 34g

36. Sun-Dried Tomato and Feta Bread

- Prep time: 20 min
- Cooking Time: 2 hours 30 min
- Serving: 1 loaf

Ingredients:

- 2 and half-cup of bread flour
- 1-cup of hot water
- 1 package dry active yeast
- Olive oil, 1/4 cup.
- 1/3 cup of chopped sun-dried tomatoes and 1/2 cup of feta cheese.
- one tablespoon dried basil
- one-half teaspoon of garlic powder

Directions:

1. The yeast should be dissolved in warm water and given five minutes to proof.
2. Olive oil, feta cheese, sun-dried tomatoes, basil, and garlic powder should all be combined.
3. Add the bread flour gradually while kneading the dough until it is smooth.
4. For about an hour, the dough should rise covered until it has doubled in size.
5. Select the Basic or White Bread setting on your breadmaker.
6. Place the dough in the bread pan after shaping it.
7. Allow the dough to rise in the pan for 30 more minutes.
8. The bread should be baked until the top is golden and the loaf shakes when tapped.
9. Prior to slicing, let the bread cool.

Nutritional Information:

- Kcal: 210
- Protein: 6g
- Fat: 7g
- Carbs: 32g

37. Fragrant Herb Bread

- Makes: 2 lb. / 900 g/16 slices
- Cook Time: 3½ hours.

Ingredients:

- 450 grams (four cups) of low-carb bread mixture
- ¾ cup (180 ml) of lukewarm (90°F/32°C) water
- 180 g or ¾ cup of heavy cream
- Beaten medium egg
- Avocado oil, 2 tablespoons
- 2 Tbsp (27 g) Xylitol
- Dry thyme, 1 tablespoon
- dried basil, 1 tablespoon
- garlic powder, 1/2 tsp.
- 1 ½ tablespoons instant yeast

Directions:

1. The bread maker bucket should now contain the wet ingredients.
2. Make a well on top of the liquids and add all the dry ingredients.
3. Spread the yeast throughout the area and cover it with honey or sugar to feed it.
4. Put the bread maker's lid on and select the 3-hour BASIC/WHITE BREAD/LOW-CARB program.
5. Use a spatula to aid the bread maker in forming a ball because the gluten-free dough requires a lot of work to knead. Likewise, alter the dough's liquid content. The final product will resemble a brick if the ideal ball with the proper texture doesn't emerge.
6. After baking, let the bread cool for an hour on a rack before slicing and serving.

Nutrition Facts (Per Serving):

- Kcal 98.
- Carbs 4.3 g,
- Fat 4.6 g;
- Carb 10.5 g;
- Protein 3.4 g

38. French Bread

- Makes: 1½ lb./700 g/12 slices
- Cook Time: 3½ hours.

Ingredients:

- 1 cup (100 g) of almond flour
- ½ cup of oat fiber
- 1 cup (125 g) of vital wheat gluten
- 1 cup (250 ml) of lukewarm water (90°F/32°C)
- 3 medium eggs (room temperature), beaten
- ⅓ cup (80 g) of unsalted butter, softened
- ½ tsp. of xanthan gum
- 5 Tbsp. (43 g) of erythritol
- 1 tsp. of honey
- ½ tsp. of kosher salt
- 1½ Tbsp. of instant yeast

Directions:

1. The bread maker bucket should now contain the wet ingredients.
2. Make a well on top of the liquids and add all the dry ingredients.
3. Spread the yeast throughout the area and cover it with honey or sugar to feed it.
4. Put the bread maker's lid on and select the 3-hour BASIC/WHITE BREAD/LOW-CARB program.
5. Use a spatula to aid the bread maker in forming a ball because the gluten-free dough requires a lot of work to knead. Likewise, alter the dough's liquid content. The final product will resemble a brick if the ideal ball with the proper texture doesn't emerge.

6. After baking, let the bread cool for an hour on a rack before slicing and serving.

Nutrition Facts (Per Serving):

- Kcal 152;
- Carbs 9.2 g, To
- Fat 8.4 g;
- Carb 10.6 g;
- Protein 9.2 g

39. Mediterranean Herb and Cheese Breadsticks

- Prep time: 25 min
- Cook time: 15 min.
- Serving: 12 breadsticks

Ingredients:

- 2 ½ cups of bread flour
- 1-cup of hot water
- ¼ cup olive oil ¼ cup grated Parmesan cheese 1 packet active dry yeast
- 1 tablespoon dried thyme from Italy (oregano, thyme, rosemary)
- 1 teaspoon of powdered garlic
- ½ tsp. sea salt

Directions:

1. The yeast should be dissolved in warm water and given five minutes to proof.
2. Add the sea salt, dried Italian herbs, garlic powder, and grated Parmesan cheese to the mixture.
3. Add the bread flour gradually while kneading the dough until it is smooth.
4. For about an hour, the dough should rise covered until it has doubled in size.
5. Set your breadmaker to the Dough or Manual setting to preheat.
6. Roll the dough into 12 sticks after dividing it into portions.
7. The sticks should be placed on a baking sheet and left to cool for 15 minutes.
8. Bake the breadsticks in a preheated oven until they are golden brown.
9. Serve hot.

Nutritional Information:

- Kcal: 170
- Protein: 5g
- Fat: 5g
- Carbs: 25g

40. Focaccia with Cheese

- Makes: 1 tortilla
- Cook Time: ½ hour
- Program: Dough

Ingredients:

- ¼ cup (30 g) of almond flour
- 1 cup (100 g) of mozzarella cheese, shredded and melted.
- 1 Tbsp. of cream cheese
- 1 medium egg, slightly beaten.
- 2 minced garlic cloves
- 1/2 teaspoon dried rosemary
- 1/2 teaspoon dried sage
- 1 teaspoon dried basil, 1/4 teaspoon pink salt, and 1/4 teaspoon black pepper

Directions:

1. The bread maker bucket should now contain the wet ingredients.
2. The dry ingredients should be layered on top of the liquids.
3. Put the bread maker's lid on and select the DOUGH setting.
4. Use a spatula to aid the bread maker in forming a ball because the gluten-free dough requires a lot of work to knead. Likewise, alter the dough's liquid content. The final product will resemble a brick if the ideal ball with the proper texture doesn't emerge.
5. In the interim, heat the oven to 350°F (180°C).
6. Create a flatbread on the baking sheet once the dough has been kneaded.
7. Bake it for 10 to 15 minutes, or until golden brown.
8. After baking, let the bread cool for an hour on a rack before slicing and serving.

Nutrition Facts:

- Kcal 353;
- Carbs 7.2 g,
- Fat 27.3 g;
- Carb 11.1 g;
- Protein 20.7 g

41. Olive Oregano Focaccia

- Makes: 9 servings
- Cook Time: ¾ hour
- Program: Dough

Ingredients:

- 1½ cups (5.3 oz., 150 g) of almond flour
- 1½ (200 g) cups of mozzarella, melted
- 1 oz. (28 g) of cream cheese, softened
- 1 medium egg, beaten
- 1 Tbsp. dried oregano/rosemary/basil
- 2 Tbsp. black olives, chopped (for topping)
- olive oil spray
- ½ tsp. of coarse sea salt (for topping)
- 1 Tbsp. of keto baking powder

Directions:

1. Put wet ingredients in the bread maker bucket.
2. Place all dry ingredients on top of fluids.
3. Close the lid and set the bread maker to DOUGH.
4. Since gluten-free dough is hard to knead, help the bread maker form a ball with a spatula. Adjust the dough's liquid. If the perfect ball with the right texture doesn't come out, the product looks like a brick.
5. Meanwhile, heat the oven to 350°F (180°C).
6. Knead the dough and make a flatbread on the baking sheet. Press olives on top. Season with coarse sea salt. Dress with olive oil.
7. Bake 10-15 minutes until golden brown.

8. After baking, let bread cool on a rack for ⅓ hour before serving.

Nutrition Facts (Per Serving):

- Kcal 154;
- Carbs 3.2 g,
- Fat 13.2 g;
- Carb 4.8 g
- Protein 10.1 g

42. Italian Keto Bread

- Prep Time: 10 minutes
- Cook Time: 50 minutes
- Makes: 2 lb./900 g/16 slices

Ingredients:

- 1 Tbsp. of coconut flour
- 2½ cups (240 g) of almond flour
- 2 Tbsp. of unflavored protein isolate
- ½ cup (120 g) of unsalted and softened butter
- 1½ tsp. of keto baking powder
- 8 oz. (230 g) of full-fat cream (softened)
- 9 room temperature eggs, beaten
- 1 tsp. of rosemary
- 1 tsp. of marjoram
- 3 tsp. of oregano
- 2 Tbsp. of garlic powder (or 3 minced garlic cloves)

Directions:

1. Add the wet ingredients to a bread machine bucket.
2. Lastly, add the dry ingredients—the almond flour, the coconut flour, and the unflavored protein isolate into the egg mixture.
3. Set the program to QUICK BREAD.
4. You can add all herbs and spices along with dry ingredients or after the signal.

5. After the kneading cycle, make sure everything is evenly combined. You are looking for a smooth consistency.
6. Allow it to bake for around 45–50 minutes until the bread becomes golden brown, checking with a toothpick.

Nutrition Facts (per serving):

- Kcal 180,
- Carbs 3 g,
- Fat 15 g,
- Protein 5 g,

43. Italian Keto Breadsticks

- Cook Time: 15 minutes.
- Makes: 16 sticks

Ingredients:

- 1½ cups (140 g) almond flour
- 2½ cups (280 g) shredded mozzarella cheese
- 2 eggs
- oz. (85 g) cream cheese
- 2 tablespoons grated Parmesan
- 2 cloves garlic (you want it minced)
- 1 tablespoon psyllium husk powder
- 2 tsp keto baking powder
- 1 tablespoon nutritional yeast
- 1 tsp garlic salt
- 2 tsp dried thyme
- ½ tsp dried basil
- some flavorless olive oil to brush the tops

Directions:

1. Start by preheating the oven to 400°F (204°C). Put mozzarella and cream cheese in a microwave-safe bowl. Cook it for about 1 minute in the microwave. Stir and microwave the cheese mixture until melted.

2. Put the almond flour, psyllium husk powder, garlic salt, nutritional yeast, basil, parsley, and baking powder in a separate bowl. Fresh garlic and eggs in mozzarella. Make sure everything is mixed.
3. Add Parmesan to the cheese dough, then the dry ingredients you mixed earlier. The cheese will become sticky and hard to mix as it cools. If you're having trouble, microwave it for 10 seconds and mix again.
4. Oil your hands to handle sticky dough. Cut the dough into 8 pieces. Shape dough into logs and cut into 16 breadsticks. Place these rolls on a parchment-lined baking sheet. Bake it for 12 minutes on the top rack. Remember to rotate the pan halfway through.
5. Brush olive oil on the breadsticks after removing them from the oven. Bake for another 3 minutes. It should cool slightly before serving and enjoying!

Nutrition Facts (per serving):

- Kcal 115,
- Carbs 4 g,
- Fat 6 g,
- Protein 10 g

44. Keto Garlic Butter Bread

- Prep Time: 10 minutes
- Cook Time: 35 minutes
- Makes: 16 buns

Ingredients:

- 280 g (2½ cups) mozzarella (shredded)
- 60 g cream cheese (2)
- 3. Slightly beaten eggs
- 140 g (1½ cups) almond flour
- keto baking powder 1 tsp
- cooked bacon bits (20 g) ⅓ cup
- 1/6 cup (60 g) Parmesan (grated)
- French herb (1 tsp)
- 1/4 cup (60 g) browned butter
- 4 minced garlic cloves

- Add ½ cup chopped fresh parsley.

Directions:

1. Grease a medium cast iron with oil/butter or cooking spray and set it aside. Mix French herbs and Parmesan on a shallow plate.
2. Melt mozzarella and cream cheese in a large bowl for 1 minute in the microwave. Mix well until smooth.
3. Mix melted cheese, eggs, baking powder, bacon, and almond flour. Combine everything to make a smooth batter.
4. Roll the dough in Italian seasoning and Parmesan with a large cookie scoop. Place it in your prepared skillet. Sprinkle Parmesan cheese on top after filling the pan. Put the skillet in the fridge for 10 minutes.
5. Start by preheating the oven to 400°F (200°C).
6. Remove the skillet from the fridge and bake the garlic-butter bread for 20–25 minutes. The finished product should be golden brown.
7. Then mince the garlic and mix it with the parsley and browned butter in a small bowl.
8. Brush a generous amount of butter/garlic sauce on keto bread after baking.

Nutrition Facts (per serving):

- Kcal 238,
- Carbs 10.11 g,
- Fat 36.42 g,
- Protein 43.9 g

45. Greek Yogurt Keto Bread

- Prep Time: 10 minutes
- Cook Time: 1½ hours
- Makes: 1½ lb./700 g/12 servings

Ingredients:

- ¾ cup (180 ml) of full-fat Greek yogurt
- 4 large room temperature eggs, beaten
- ½ cup (120 ml) of melted butter

- 1 cup almond flour
- 1 cup sesame flour
- 4 Tbsp flaxseed meal
- 1 Tbsp psyllium husk powder
- 1 tsp. salt
- 1 tbsp apple cider vinegar
- 1 tsp baking soda

Topping:

- 2 Tbsp. of chopped walnuts
- 2 Tbsp. of poppy seeds

Directions:

1. Fill the bread machine pan with yogurt. Add other ingredients. (Per manufacturer's instructions).
2. Allow your bread machine to do the KNEAD/DOUGH bread cycle until the dough has been mixed and ready to bake. Before it bakes, sprinkle the walnuts and poppy seeds—lightly tap them so they stick to the bread.
3. Allow the bread machine to continue the BAKING cycle (the rising cycle is unnecessary as it uses baking soda).
4. Allow the bread to cool before you slice it. Store it at room temperature.

Nutritious Facts (per serving):

- Kcal: 211,
- Carbs 4.9 g,
- Fat 17.5 g,
- Protein 9 g

Chapter 7:
Whole Wheat Bread

- **Cook time:** 15 minutes
- **Servings:** 10

Ingredients:

- 1 1/8 cups warm water (110/45 C)
- 3 tbsp honey
- 1/3 tsp salt ½ cups whole wheat flour
- 1 ½ cups bread flour
- 2 Tbsp vegetable oil
- ½ tsp dry active yeast

Directions:

1. Put ingredients in bread machine in manufacturer-recommended order.
2. Select Wheat Bread and Light Color on the machine.

Nutrition:

- Kcal: 180
- Carb: 33.4 g
- Fat: 3.5 g
- Protein: 5.2 g

47. Cornmeal Whole Wheat Bread

- **Cook time:** 30 minutes
- **Servings:** 10

Ingredients:

- 2 ½ tsps. Active dry yeast
- 1 1/3 cups Water
- 2 tbsps. Sugar
- 1, lightly beaten Egg
- 2 tbsps. Butter
- 1 ½ tsps. Salt
- ¾ cup. Cornmeal
- ¾ cup. Whole wheat flour
- 2 ¾ cups. Bread flour

Directions:

1. Add all ingredients to the bread machine pan per manufacturer's instructions.
2. Set basic bread, then medium crust, and start.
3. Remove the loaf pan from the machine after baking.
4. Let it cool for 10 minutes. Slice and serve.

Nutrition:

- Kcal 228,
- Carbs 41.2 g
- Fat 3.3 g
- Protein 7.1 g

48. Oat and Honey Whole Wheat Bread

- **Cook time:** 15 minutes.
- **Servings:** 10

Ingredients:

- Buttermilk, one cup
- 1 egg
- A quarter cup of warm water (110°F/45°C)
- 1 ½ cups of whole wheat flour, 2 tablespoons of honey
- All-purpose flour, 1 ½ cups
- Quick-cooking oats in a cup
- Vegetable oil, two tablespoons
- Salt and active dry yeast in a ratio of 1 ½ teaspoons each

Directions:

1. Verify all ingredients, then add them to the bread maker as directed by the manufacturer.
2. Choose Whole Wheat or Light Crust. Click "Start."

Nutrition:

- Kcal: 200
- Carb: 35 g
- Total Fat: 4.3 g
- Protein: 6.6 g

49. Maple Whole Wheat Bread

- **Cook time:** 15 minutes.
- **Servings:** 10

Ingredients:

- 2 and a half cups whole wheat flour
- 50 g of bread flour

- 1 ¼ cups of water, 1/3 teaspoon of salt
- Maple syrup, 4 tablespoons
- 1 ½ teaspoons active dry yeast, 2 tablespoons olive oil

Directions:

1. In the order recommended by the manufacturer, add the ingredients to the bread machine pan.
2. On the machine, select the Wheat Bread cycle, and then press the Start button.

Nutrition:

- Kcal: 144
- Carb: 26.9 g
- Fat: 2.8 g
- Protein: 4.3 g

50. 100 Percent Whole-Wheat Bread

- **Prep time:** 10 minutes or less
- **Cook time: 45 minutes.**
- **Servings:** 10

Ingredients

8 slices / 1 pound

- ¾ cup water, between 80° and 90°F
- 1 ½ tablespoons of cooled, melted butter.
- Honey, 1 ½ tablespoons
- ¼ cup salt
- Whole-wheat bread flour, two cups
- 1 teaspoon instant or bread machine yeast

12 slices / 1½ pounds

- 1.8 cups water, between 80° and 90°F
- 2 ¼ tablespoons cooled, melted butter.
- Honey, 2 tablespoons

- Salt, 1.8 teaspoons
- Whole-wheat bread flour, 3 cups
- 1 ½ teaspoons instant or bread machine yeast

16 slices / 2 pounds

- 1 ½ cups water, between 80 and 90 °F
- 3 tablespoons cooled, melted butter.
- honey, 3 tablespoons
- 3. 4 cups whole-wheat bread flour, 1 ½ teaspoons of salt
- 2 teaspoons instant or bread machine yeast

Directions

1. Following the manufacturer's instructions, add the ingredients to your bread maker.
2. Select a light or medium crust, program the machine for whole-wheat/whole-grain bread, and then hit Start.
3. Remove the bucket from the machine once the loaf is finished baking.
4. Give the loaf five minutes to cool.
5. To remove the loaf and turn it out onto a rack to cool, gently shake the bucket.
6. Have You Heard? Unlike white flour, which only contains the endosperm, whole-wheat flour contains the endosperm, bran, and germ of the wheat berry. This indicates that whole-wheat flour is very nutrient-dense and rich in beneficial fiber, vitamins, and minerals.

Nutrition:

- Kcal: 146
- Fat: 3 g
- Carbs: 27 g
- Protein: 3g

- **Cook time:** 15 minutes.
- **Servings:** 12

Ingredients:

- 1 and a half cups buttermilk
- 1 ½ tablespoons of melted butter
- White sugar, 2 tablespoons
- ¼ teaspoon of salt
- 3 cups regular flour
- 30 grams of whole wheat flour
- 1.5 teaspoons dry active yeast

Directions:

1. Measure each ingredient in the bread maker pan according to the manufacturer's recommended sequence. Select the Basic White Bread setting on the machine. Launch the device.
2. If the mixture does not form a ball after a few minutes or if it is too loose, add a little more buttermilk or flour.

Nutrition:

- Kcal: 160
- Carb: 30 g
- Fat: 2.1 g
- Protein: 4.9 g

- **Cook time:** 15 minutes.
- **Servings:** 12

Ingredients:

- 1.4 cups of water
- 2 tablespoons softened margarine
- 2 tablespoons of powdered dry milk
- Brown sugar, 2 tablespoons
- Salt, 1 ¼ teaspoons
- bread flour, 3 cups
- 30 grams of whole wheat flour
- 1/fourth cup cracked wheat
- Active dry yeast, 1 1/4 teaspoons

Directions:

1. Measure each ingredient in the bread machine pan according to the manufacturer's recommended order.
2. Select the regular or light cycle, then begin.

Nutrition:

- Kcal: 50
- Carb: 7.3 g
- Fat: 1.9 g
- Protein: 1.4 g

- **Cook time:** 15 minutes
- **Servings:** 12

Ingredients:

- one water cup
- 2 tablespoons of butter
- Honey, two tablespoons
- bread flour, 2 cups
- a half-cup of whole wheat flour
- 1/3 cup powdered dry milk.
- 1 salt shakerful
- 1 (.25 oz.) packaged dry active yeast

Directions:

1. Put the ingredients in the bread maker according to the manufacturer's suggested order. Use the Wheat setting on the breadmaker to produce a large loaf (1-1/2 lbs).

Nutrition:

- Kcal: 57
- Carb: 8.5 g
- Total Fat: 1.9 g
- Protein: 2.1 g

54. Classic Whole Wheat Bread

- **Cook time:** 1 hour 30 minutes.

Ingredients:

- ¼ slices of bread (2 pounds)
- one cup of warm water
- 2 eggs, at room temperature, melted in ½ cup unsalted butter.
- ¼ cup sugar, 2 teaspoons table salt

- Whole-wheat flour, 1 ½ cups
- White bread flour, 2 ½ cups
- 2 teaspoons yeast for bread machine
- (12 slices; 11.2 pounds)
- 3.5 ounces of warm water
- 2 eggs, at room temperature, melted in 1/3 cup unsalted butter.
- ½ -tablespoons of salt
- sugar, 3 tablespoons
- Whole-wheat flour, 1 cup.
- White bread flour, 2 cups
- 1.3 teaspoons of bread maker yeast

Directions:

1. Decide on the loaf size you want to make, then weigh out your ingredients.
2. In the order given above, add the ingredients to the bread pan.
3. Put the pan inside the bread maker and secure the top.
4. Activate the bread maker. Choose either the White/Basic or Whole Wheat/ Whole Grain setting; both are suitable for this recipe. Choose the loaf size next, and then the color of the crust. launch the cycle.
5. Carefully take the pan out of the oven once the cycle is complete and the bread is baked. Because the handle will be extremely hot, use a potholder. Allow me to rest for a while.
6. Before slicing, take the bread out of the pan and let it cool on a wire rack for at least 10 minutes.

Nutrition:

- Kcal: 176
- Fat: 5.3 g
- Carbs: 24.2 g
- Protein: 5.2 g

- **Cook time:** 1 hour 30 minutes
- **Servings:** 10

Ingredients

8 slices / 1 pound

- ½ cup water, between 80° and 90°F
- ¼ cup milk, 80°F
- 2 teaspoons cooled, melted butter.
- 1 tablespoon molasses and 2 tablespoons honey
- 1 tablespoon skim milk powder and 1 teaspoon sugar
- Salt, ½ teaspoon
- Unsweetened cocoa powder, 1 teaspoon
- Whole-wheat flour, 1 ¼ cups
- 1 cup of bread flour, white
- 1 teaspoon instant or bread machine yeast

12 slices / 1½ pounds

- ¾ cup water, between 80° and 90°F
- 1/3 cup milk, 80 °F
- 1 tablespoon cooled, melted butter.
- 34 teaspoons of honey
- molasses, two tablespoons
- sugar, 2 teaspoons
- 2 tablespoons of powdered skim milk
- ¼ cup salt
- unsweetened cocoa powder, 2 teaspoons
- Whole-wheat flour, 3.5 cups
- White bread flour, 1 ¼ cups
- 1.8 teaspoons instant or bread machine yeast

16 slices / 2 pounds

- 1 cup water, between 80° and 90°F

- ½ cup milk, 80°F
- 2 tablespoons cooled, melted butter.
- 3 tablespoons molasses, 5 tablespoons honey.
- 1 teaspoon of sugar
- 3 tablespoons of powdered skim milk
- 1 salt shakerful
- Unsweetened cocoa powder, 1 tablespoon
- Whole-wheat flour, 2 ½ cups
- White bread flour, 2 cups
- 1 ½ teaspoons instant or bread machine yeast

Directions

1. Following the manufacturer's instructions, add the ingredients to your bread maker.
2. Choose a light or medium crust, program the machine for Basic/White bread, and then hit Start.
3. Remove the bucket from the machine once the loaf is finished baking.
4. Give the loaf five minutes to cool.
5. To remove the loaf and turn it out onto a rack to cool, gently shake the bucket.

Nutrition:

- Kcal: 164
- Fat: 2 g
- Carbs: 34 g
- Protein: 4 g

Chapter 8:
Spice, Nut & Herb Bread

56. Spicy Cajun Bread

- Servings: 1 Loaf
- Cook time: 10 Minutes.

Ingredients:

- (12 slices; 1.2 pounds)
- 1.8 cups water, between 80° and 90°F
- 1 ½ tablespoons of cooled, melted butter
- 1/fourth cup tomato paste
- 1 ½ teaspoons salt and 1 ½ tablespoons sugar
- 3 tablespoons of powdered skim milk
- ¼ cup Cajun seasoning
- ¼ cup onion powder
- 3 cups bread flour, white
- 1 ¼ teaspoons instant or bread machine yeast

Directions:

1. Getting the Ingredients Ready.
2. Measure the ingredients after selecting the desired loaf size.
3. All the previously listed ingredients should be added.
4. After inserting the pan into the bread maker, secure the lid.
5. choose the Bake cycle.
6. Start the bread maker. Choose the loaf size, the crust color, and the White/Basic setting. Start by pressing the button.
7. Carefully remove the pan from the bread maker after the cycle is complete, then leave it to cool.
8. Bread should be taken out of the pan and placed on a wire rack to cool for about 10 minutes. Slice

Nutrition:

- Kcal: 105.8.
- Fat: 6.8 g;
- Carbs: 2.3 g;
- Protein: 9.6 g

57. Rosemary Cranberry Pecan Bread

- Servings: 14 Slices
- Cook time: 3 H.

Ingredients:

- 1⅓ cups water, plus
- 1 Tbsp water
- 2 tbsp. butter
- 2 teaspoons of salt
- bread flour, 4 cups
- ¾ cup dried sweetened cranberries
- ¾ cup toasted chopped pecans
- 2 Tbsp non-fat powdered milk
- ¼ cup sugar
- 2 tsp yeast

Directions:

1. According to the manufacturer's instructions, put each ingredient into the bread maker in the right amount at the right temperature.
2. On your bread maker, close the lid, choose the basic bread, medium crust setting, and hit start.
3. Take out the bread and place it on a cooling rack after the bread maker has finished baking.

Nutrition:

- Kcal: 105
- Fat: 6 g

- Carbs: 2 g
- Protein: 9 g

58. Basic Pecan Bread

- Servings: 1 Loaf

Ingredients:

- 14 slices of bread (2 pounds)
- 1 1/3 ounces of warm milk
- 1 egg, melted in 22.3 tablespoons of unsalted butter, served at room temperature.
- Sugar, 2 ¾ tablespoons
- Table salt, 1 1/3 teaspoons
- White bread flour, 4 cups
- 2 teaspoons yeast for bread machines
- 1.3 cups toasted pecans, chopped.
- (12 slices; 1.2 pounds)
- 1 glass of warm milk
- 1 egg, melted in 2 tablespoons of unsalted butter, at room temperature.
- two teaspoons of sugar
- 1 tablespoon of salt
- 3 cups bread flour, white
- 1 ½ teaspoons yeast for bread machine
- 1 cup toasted, chopped pecans.

Directions:

1. Decide on the loaf size you want to make, then weigh out your ingredients.
2. In the order mentioned above, add all of the ingredients to the bread pan minus the toasted pecans.
3. Put the pan inside the breadmaker and secure the top.
4. Activate the breadmaker. Choose the loaf size, then the White/Basic or Fruit/Nut setting (if your machine has these options), and finally the color of the crust. launch the cycle.
5. Add the toasted pecans when the machine says to add ingredients. (Some machines allow you to start the machine with toasted pecans added to a fruit or

nut hopper. During baking, the machine will automatically incorporate them into the dough.)

6. Carefully take the pan out of the oven once the cycle is complete and the bread is baked. Because the handle will be extremely hot, use a potholder. Allow to rest for a while.

7. Before slicing, take the bread out of the pan and let it cool on a wire rack for at least 10 minutes.

Nutritional Information (Per Serving):

- Kcal 168,
- fat 4.8 g,
- carbs 25.6 g,
- protein 5 g

59. Whole Wheat Raisin Bread

- Servings: 10
- Cook time: 2 Hours.

Ingredients:

- 3.5 cups whole wheat flour
- 2 teaspoons dry yeast.
- 2 lightly beaten eggs
- 1-fourth cup softened butter
- 3/4 cup of water
- 1/3 cup milk
- Salt: 1 teaspoon.
- 1/3 cup sugar
- 4 teaspoons of cinnamon.
- Cinnamon - 1 cup.

Directions:

1. Fill the bread pan with water, milk, butter, and eggs. To the bread pan, add the remaining ingredients without the yeast. With your finger, poke a tiny hole in the flour and pour the yeast into it.

2. Make sure that no liquids will be mixed with the yeast. Choose the whole wheat setting, then click the light/medium crust button to begin.
3. Remove the loaf pan from the oven once the loaf has finished baking. Ten minutes of cooling is appropriate. Slice, then dish.

Nutrition:

- Kcal: 110
- Fat: 7 g
- Carbs: 4 g
- Protein: 9 g

60. Toasted Pecan Bread

- Servings: 1 Loaf
- Cook time: 10 Minutes.

Ingredients:

- (12 slices; 1.2 pounds)
- 1 cup milk, between 70° and 80°F
- 2 tablespoons cooled, melted butter.
- At room temperature, one egg

- two teaspoons of sugar
- 1 salt shakerful
- 3 cups bread flour, white
- 1 ½ teaspoons instant or bread machine yeast
- 1 cup toasted, chopped pecans.

Directions:

1. Getting the Ingredients Ready.
2. In the order and at the temperature advised by the manufacturer of your bread machine, add all the ingredients to the bread maker except the pecans and raisins.
3. choose the Bake cycle.
4. Choose a light or medium crust, program the machine for Basic/White bread, and then hit Start.
5. Add the pecans or place them in a nut/raisin hopper and the machine will add them automatically when it signals.
6. Carefully remove the pan from the bread maker after the cycle is complete, then leave it to cool.
7. Bread should be taken out of the pan and placed on a wire rack to cool for about 5 minutes. Slice

Nutrition:

- Kcal: 115
- Fat: 4 g
- Carbs: 2 g
- Protein: 10 g

- Servings: 6 Pcs
- Cook time: 15 Minutes

Ingredients:

- 2 tablespoons of coconut flour per 1/2 cup.
- Baking soda, a pinch of salt
- one tablespoon of flax meal
- 2 tablespoons of coconut oil.
- Cilantro chopped, and a cup of warm water

Directions:

1. In a bowl, combine the salt, baking soda, flax, and coconut flour.
2. Add the chopped cilantro, water, and coconut oil.
3. Knead it until a smooth dough forms out of everything.
4. Give yourself about 15 minutes to rest.
5. Divide the dough into six portions of the same size.
6. Each of them should be formed into a ball, which you should then flatten with a rolling pin between parchment paper.
7. Keep chilled until you're ready to use.
8. Heat for two to three minutes on each side in a nonstick pan to cook.

Nutrition Info:

- Kcal 46.
- Fat: 4 g
- Protein: 1 g.
- Carbs: 1 g.

- Servings: 1 Loaf
- Cook time: 10 Minutes.

Ingredients:

- 16 pieces of bread (2 pounds)
- 1 ½ cups milk, between 80° and 90°F
- 2 tablespoons cooled, melted butter.
- 2 teaspoons salt and 2 tablespoons sugar
- two teaspoons of freshly chopped lavender flowers.
- Lemon zest, 1 teaspoon; fresh thyme, ½ teaspoon, chopped.
- White bread flour, 4 cups
- 1 ½ teaspoons instant or bread machine yeast

Directions:

1. Getting the Ingredients Ready.
2. Measure the ingredients after selecting the desired loaf size.
3. All the previously listed ingredients should be added.
4. After inserting the pan into the bread maker, secure the lid.
5. choose the Bake cycle.
6. Start the bread maker. Choose the loaf size, the crust color, and the White/Basic setting. Start by pressing the button.
7. Carefully remove the pan from the bread maker after the cycle is complete, then leave it to cool.
8. Bread should be taken out of the pan and placed on a wire rack to cool for about 10 minutes. Slice

Nutrition:

- Kcal: 105
- Fat: 6 g
- Carbs: 2 g
- Protein: 9 g

- Servings: 22 Slices
- Cook time: 1 Hour

Ingredients:

- 1 ½ cups lukewarm water (80 degrees F)
- Two tablespoons sugar
- Three teaspoons active dry yeast
- 4 ½ cups wheat flour
- One whole egg
- Two teaspoons kosher salt
- One tablespoon olive oil
- Three small onions, chopped and lightly toasted
- 1 cup bacon, chopped

Directions:

1. Prepare all the bread ingredients and the measuring tools (a cup, a spoon, kitchen scales).
2. With the exception of the bacon and onion, carefully measure the ingredients into the pan.
3. In accordance with the instructions in your bread machine's manual, add all the ingredients to a bucket in the correct order.
4. Put the cover on.
5. Your bread maker's program should be set to BASIC, and the crust color should be MEDIUM.
6. Select START.
7. Add the onion and bacon after the machine beeps.
8. Hold off until the program is finished.
9. When finished, remove the bucket, and allow it to cool for five to ten minutes.
10. Shake the loaf out of the pan and place it on a cooling rack to cool for 30 minutes.
11. Sliced, served, and tasting delicious homemade bread.

Nutrition Info:

- Kcal: 391 Cal;

- Fat: 9.7 g;
- Carbs: 59.9 g;
- Protein 3.4g

64. Market Seed Bread

- Servings: 1 Loaf
- Cook time: 10 Minutes

Ingredients:

- (12 slices; 1.2 pounds)
- 80° to 90°F, 1 cup plus 2 tablespoons milk.
- 1 ½ tablespoons of cooled, melted butter.
- 34 teaspoon salt, 1 ½ tablespoons honey
- flaxseed, 3 tablespoons
- Sesame seeds, 3 tablespoons
- Poppy seeds, 1 ½ tablespoons
- Whole-wheat flour, 1 ¼ cups
- White bread flour, 1.5 cups
- 1.5 teaspoons instant or bread machine yeast

Directions:

1. Measure the ingredients after selecting the desired loaf size.
2. All of the previously listed ingredients should be added.
3. After inserting the pan into the bread maker, secure the lid.
4. choose the Bake cycle.
5. Start the bread maker. Choose the loaf size, the crust color, and the White/Basic setting. Start by pressing the button.
6. Carefully remove the pan from the bread maker after the cycle is complete, then leave it to cool.
7. Bread should be taken out of the pan and placed on a wire rack to cool for about 5 minutes. Slice

Nutrition:

- Kcal: 105

- Fat: 6 g
- Carbs: 2 g
- Protein: 9 g

65. Pumpkin Pie Spice Bread

- Servings: 12
- Cook time: 1 Hour And 20 Minutes

Ingredients:

- ½ cup brown sugar
- ½ cup white sugar
- 1 cup of canned pumpkin
- 1/3 cup oil
- Vanilla: 1 teaspoon.
- 2 eggs 1 ½ cups all-purpose flour
- 2 teaspoons of baking powder.
- ¼ teaspoon of salt.
- 1 ½ teaspoons of pumpkin pie spice.
- ½ cup chopped walnuts.

Directions:

1. According to the bread machine's instructions, add everything.
2. Select Medium crust and the Quick bread cycle. Click "Start."
3. When the bread is done, remove it.
4. Slice, let cool, then serve.

Nutrition Info: (Per Serving):

- Kcal: 225.
- Fat: 10 g;
- Carbs: 31 g;
- Protein: 4 g

- Servings: 1 Loaf
- Cook time: 10 Minutes.

Ingredients:

- 16 pieces of bread (2 pounds)
- Milk, lukewarm, 1.8 cups
- At room temperature, one egg
- ¼ cup of honey and 2 teaspoons of unsalted butter
- Table salt, 1 1/3 teaspoons
- White bread, 4 cups flour
- 13 teaspoons of cardamom, ground
- 1.3 teaspoons of bread maker yeast

Directions:

1. Measure the ingredients after selecting the desired loaf size.
2. All of the previously listed ingredients should be added.
3. After inserting the pan into the breadmaker, secure the lid.
4. choose the Bake cycle.
5. Start the breadmaker. Choose the loaf size, the crust color, and the White/Basic setting. Start by pressing the button.
6. Carefully remove the pan from the bread maker after the cycle is complete, then leave it to cool.
7. Bread should be taken out of the pan and placed on a wire rack to cool for about 10 minutes. Slice

- Servings: 1 Loaf
- Cook time: 10 Minutes.

Ingredients:

- (12 slices; 1.2 pounds)
- 80° to 90°F, 1 cup plus 2 tablespoons of water
- 2 tablespoons cooled, melted butter
- Honey, 1 ½ tablespoons
- Salt, 1 ½ teaspoons
- 2 tablespoons and 1 cup of multigrain flour
- White bread flour, 2 cups
- 1 ½ teaspoons active dry yeast or bread machine

Directions:

1. Measure the ingredients after selecting the desired loaf size.
2. All of the previously listed ingredients should be added.
3. After inserting the pan into the breadmaker, secure the lid.
4. choose the Bake cycle.
5. Start the breadmaker. Choose the loaf size, the crust color, and the White/Basic setting. Start by pressing the button.
6. Carefully remove the pan from the bread maker after the cycle is complete, then leave it to cool.
7. Bread should be taken out of the pan and placed on a wire rack to cool for about 5 minutes. Slice

Nutrition:

- Kcal: 105
- Fat: 6 g
- Carbs: 2 g
- Protein: 9 g

- Servings: 1 Loaf
- Cook time: 10 Minutes.

Ingredients:

- (12 slices; 1.2 pounds)
- 1 cup water, between 80° and 90°F
- At room temperature, one egg
- 3 tablespoons cooled, melted butter.
- 3 tablespoons of powdered skim milk
- Honey, 1 ½ tablespoons
- Salt, 1 ½ teaspoons
- raw sunflower seeds, ¼ cup
- 3 cups bread flour, white
- 1 teaspoon instant or bread machine yeast

Directions:

1. Measure the ingredients after selecting the desired loaf size.
2. All of the previously listed ingredients should be added.
3. After inserting the pan into the breadmaker, secure the lid.
4. choose the Bake cycle.
5. Start the breadmaker. Choose the loaf size, the crust color, and the White/Basic setting. Start by pressing the button.
6. Carefully remove the pan from the bread maker after the cycle is complete, then leave it to cool.
7. Bread should be taken out of the pan and placed on a wire rack to cool for about 5 minutes. Slice

Nutrition:

- Kcal: 111
- Fat: 5 g
- Carbs: 2 g
- Protein: 12 g

- Servings: 1 Loaf
- Cook time: 10 Minutes.

Ingredients:

- (12 slices; 1.2 pounds)
- ¼ cup of hot water
- Bulgur wheat, 3 tablespoons
- Quick oats, 3 tablespoons
- at room temperature, two eggs
- 112 tablespoons of cooled, melted butter.
- Honey, 2 tablespoons
- 1 salt shakerful
- White bread flour, 24 cups
- 1 ½ teaspoons instant or bread machine yeast

Directions:

1. Your bread maker's bucket should contain water, bulgur, and oats. Set the timer for 30 minutes or until the liquid reaches an internal temperature of 80° to 90°F.
2. In accordance with the manufacturer's instructions, add the remaining ingredients to your breadmaker.
3. choose the Bake cycle.
4. Start the breadmaker. Choose the loaf size, the crust color, and the White/Basic setting. Start by pressing the button.
5. Carefully remove the pan from the bread maker after the cycle is complete, then leave it to cool.
6. Bread should be taken out of the pan and placed on a wire rack to cool for about 5 minutes. Slice

Nutrition:

- Kcal: 105
- Fat: 6 g
- Carbs: 2 g
- Protein: 9 g

- Servings: 14 Slices
- Cook time: 3 H.

Ingredients:

- 2.3 cups of warm-to-warm milk
- ¼ cup of water (between 70- and 80-degrees Fahrenheit)
- ¼ cup of sour cream
- 2 tbsp. butter
- ½ tsp. sugar
- 1 ½ teaspoons of salt
- bread flour, 3 cups
- 1/8 tsp. baking soda
- ¼ cup of minced chives
- 2 ¼ tsp of dry, active yeast leaves

Directions:

1. According to the manufacturer's instructions, put each ingredient into the bread maker in the right amount at the right temperature.
2. On your bread maker, close the lid, choose the basic bread, medium crust setting, and hit start.
3. Take out the bread and place it on a cooling rack after the bread maker has finished baking.

Nutrition:

- Kcal: 102
- Fat: 7 g
- Carbs: 5 g
- Protein: 13 g

Conclusion

As we draw to a satisfying conclusion our travels across the domain of the "The Bread Machine Cookbook: Your Ticket to a Gastronomic Adventure Around the World by means of the smell of bread that has just been baked "to a gratifying conclusion, it is clear that the heart of this culinary journey rests in the complementary link that exists between modernization and adherence to culinary customs. Throughout the course of our journey, we have set out on an adventure that has not only stimulated our senses but also deepened our comprehension of the bread-making process as an artistic endeavor. Let us pause for a moment to contemplate the diverse tapestry of thoughts that have been woven into these pages as we say goodbye to the comforting fragrances and the embrace of warm loaves.

This book's overarching goal is to promote an understanding that goes beyond the confines of different cultures and cuisines, much like how the aroma of freshly made bread speaks a language that is understood everywhere. Our adventure started with an in-depth investigation of the fundamentals, during which we redefined the limits of what can be accomplished by a bread machine. We embarked on a journey throughout the world, tasting the different flavors that are associated with each region while simultaneously honoring recipes that have stood the test of time. The recipes begged us to participate in a scrumptious kaleidoscope of flavors, ranging from the rustic simplicity of French baguettes to the intricate braiding of delicacies from Scandinavia.

During the course of our investigation into various methods, we dug into the mysteries of gluten, the enchantment of fermentation, and the harmonious combination of elements that may turn dough into a work of art. As we unraveled the mysteries of the factors that determine a food's consistency, flavor, and appearance, it became clear that science and art are inextricably linked. We have, with precision and clarity, deciphered the mysterious world of bread, making it possible for bakers of all levels of experience to create their own taste symphonies with their own creations.

At the beginning of this culinary adventure, a number of promises were made. These included the pledge to explore the full potential of a bread machine and to transform it into a creative instrument rather than merely a convenient appliance. As we bring the curtain down on our journey, it is abundantly evident that these promises have been kept. We have not only offered recipes, but also a culinary compass that will guide you through the complex landscape of bread-making. By fusing modern science and time-honored techniques, we have transformed the bread machine into a tool for gastronomic investigation and an instrument through which the aromatic stories of a variety of cultures can be conveyed.

As the final leg of our voyage draws to a close and the tempting aromas of our baked products begin to dissipate, there is one essential message that stands out above all others: the strong connection between nourishing food and sentimental memories. We have caught the essence of beloved memories and cultural heritage in each and every loaf and knead of bread that we make. Our kitchens have become portals to other lands as a result of the blending of different foods and cooking techniques that we have done in order to put a piece of history on our tables. This link, this capacity to span time and space via the straightforward medium of a loaf, is what we want you to take forward with you and continue to cultivate.

In conclusion, "Bread Machine Cookbook: Embark on a Culinary World Tour Through the Aromas of Freshly Baked Bread" is not merely a collection of recipes; rather, it is a celebration of the human spirit's inclination toward the act of creating and connecting. This is an homage to the time-honored custom of sitting down to a meal together and telling stories to one another. The journey that we have taken through these pages has shown us that a plain loaf has inside its golden crust the stories of countless generations, the spirit of various civilizations, and the promise of innumerable more times when people come together. I pray that the enticing scents of new experiences will always permeate your kitchens, and that your dining rooms will always be adorned with breads that go beyond their role as sources of food to become symbols of community. Toast to embracing change while maintaining respect for the past, and to relishing each mouthful of the vibrant tapestry that is life as expressed via the global language of warm, freshly baked bread!

Printed in Great Britain
by Amazon

52444368R00057